THE MODERN PRESIDENCY

THE MODERN PRESIDENCY

SIX DEBATES THAT DEFINE THE INSTITUTION

MICHAEL A. GENOVESE

Columbia University Press   *New York*

Columbia University Press
Publishers Since 1893
New York   Chichester, West Sussex
cup.columbia.edu

Copyright © 2022 Columbia University Press
All rights reserved

Library of Congress Cataloging-in-Publication Data
Names: Genovese, Michael A., author.
Title: The modern presidency : six debates that define the
institution / Michael Genovese.
Description: New York : Columbia University Press, [2022] |
Includes bibliographical references and index.
Identifiers: LCCN 2022001330 | ISBN 9780231206662 (hardback) |
ISBN 9780231206679 (trade paperback) |
ISBN 9780231556590 (ebook)
Subjects: LCSH: Presidents—United States. |
Political leadership—United States. | Executive power—
United States. | United States—Politics and government.
Classification: LCC JK516 .G44 2022 |
DDC 352.230973—dc23/eng/20220412
LC record available at https://lccn.loc.gov/2022001330

Cover design: Noah Arlow
Cover image: Getty Images

Because I couldn't decide . . . this book is dedicated to:

*1. Those who did the right thing and got crushed.
It was still worth it.*

*2. My mother and father, who gave me everything,
including the mental health issues that drove me to keep
writing books.*

*3. That smokin' hot twenty-year-old girl I could never forget
(so I married her).*

What is it like, being president of the United States? Very few ever get the chance to find out, but perhaps a short mental exercise can give us a sense of the magnitude of the burden. Think of the presidency as if it were a university, and you—the new president—walk into your first class on day one. You sit in a large lecture hall, all alone, and wait. When finally the professor walks in he says, "Let's begin."

He hands you a sheet of paper with the words "Final Examination" written at the top, and says "Okay, today— and every day for the next fourteen hundred days or so— you will take a final examination to determine your grade. I won't tell you what the subject is, and I will not hand out a reading list. I will not tell you when the exam will be given or where, and I will strictly enforce a one-hour time limit to finish and submit your answers to five essay questions. While taking the exam, the university marching band will be practicing in the back of the hall, and the cheerleaders will be working on new routines for the upcoming game. And during the exam, I will be playing my favorite head-banging heavy metal music on my 1990s 'boom-box.' Oh, and if—on any day—you receive a grade lower than an 'A,' people will likely die. Good luck."

O, it is excellent
To have a giant's strength; but it is tyrannous
To use it like a giant.

—WILLIAM SHAKESPEARE, *MEASURE FOR MEASURE*

CONTENTS

Introduction 1

1 What Is More Important, Power or Persuasion? 16

2 What Matters More, the Individual or the Institution? 29

3 Did the Framers Invent a Powerful Unitary Executive or a Limited Constitutional Office? 47

4 Which Is More Valuable, Character or Competence? 67

5 What Is More Important, Skill or Opportunity? 80

6 Will the Future of the U.S. Presidency Be One of Liberal Democracy or Illiberal Democracy? 97

Conclusion 127

Acknowledgments 139
Notes 141
Selected Bibliography 153
Index 157

THE MODERN PRESIDENCY

INTRODUCTION

W hat is the fuel that powers the American presidency? What is the secret sauce, the alchemy that the successful presidents employ but that eludes the less successful presidents? What do the winners know that the losers don't?

In the United States, with its separation of powers, checks and balances, federalism, and fragmentation of power, when a president is elected, he gains an office but not necessarily power. Power must be gained, earned, won. It is not automatically conferred. And there are other claimants to power who compete with the president: Congress, the courts, the business community, and the states to name a few.

Rulers, dictators, and authoritarians exercise power. Their will becomes law. In medieval times, the king claimed a divine right to rule, and as long as the masses accepted the myth that the king was chosen by God, the king could exercise virtually unchallenged powers.

But alas, presidents are not kings (although some presidents might wish or believe otherwise). They must work hard to gain and earn power. When elected, presidents gain office and opportunity: the office of the presidency and the opportunity to compete (from a privileged position) with others for power.

If presidents must work to gain power, they need to know how best to convert opportunity to power. What tools, resources, games, and gimmicks allow a president to become powerful? This book examines six key controversies that can help us answer this question.

My assertion that few citizens understand how the American presidency works will come as no surprise to you. But it may come as a surprise that few presidents understand how the presidency works.

That is because the office and the constitutional and political system into which it is embedded are confusing: at times contradictory, at other times vague or unclear about who shall hold and exercise power, how it should be exercised, and what checks exist to limit the office. Who declares war? Constitutionally, that power is explicitly the province of Congress. Who actually commences war? The president. Who determines the meaning and application of the Constitution on matters of separation of powers? The Supreme Court has traditionally claimed that authority, but numerous presidents have also insisted that their view of what is constitutional is just as valid as that of the Court.

Constitutional scholars often refer to the ambiguities, silences, even contradictions and paradoxes that apply to understanding presidential power. Even occupants of the White House are bedeviled in trying to explain or understand the office. Harry Truman said that "being president was like riding a tiger. A man has to keep on riding or be swallowed." Woodrow Wilson asserted that "the President is at liberty, both in law and conscience, to be as big a man as he can." Theodore Roosevelt, seeing advantage in the ambiguities inherent in the office, asserted in his autobiography that "the President as a steward of the people should take whatever action necessary for the public good unless expressly forbidden by law or the Constitution," which covers a lot of ground.[1]

But if ambiguity allows for a president to claim a wide swath of power, it also gives a less assertive president a convenient escape clause. President James Buchanan in the 1850s, paralyzed and uncertain regarding how to respond to Southern states seceding from the Union, believed that "states do not have the right to secede"; however, he further believed that he had "no constitutional power to stop them." What paralyzed Buchanan animated his successor, Abraham Lincoln.

One president paralyzed and weak, another animated and powerful. Are we talking about the same institution, the presidency? The scope of presidential claims of power—ranging from "I can do just about anything" to "I can do practically nothing"— can cause a dangerous intellectual whiplash that leaves one reeling. Could the presidency really be this protean?

In an October 1939 radio address, Winston Churchill, referring to how impenetrable the Soviet Union was, said that it was "a riddle wrapped in a mystery inside an enigma." So too it is with the American presidency. This book reveals the "hidden wiring" of the presidency. It helps readers understand what British writer Walter Bagshot referred to as the *dignified* (the pomp and reverence) and the *efficient* (how things actually work) elements of government.[2]

THE CONSTITUTION AS OUR STARTING POINT

To figure out the mystery of how presidents convert office into power, our starting point must be the Constitution. Article I deals with the Congress, and most of the key powers exercised by the government belong to Congress, from taxing to spending, war declaring to law making, commerce regulation to the forming of armies.

Article II is devoted to the executive. When compared with Article I, Article II is short and vague. Few powers are directly given to the executive, and those that are granted almost always require the Senate or someone else to *share* that power with the president (e.g., the president nominates to the Supreme Court, but all nominees must be confirmed by the Senate). Virtually all the president's powers are *shared*.

Article I consists of 2,248 words; Article II only 1,015. Brief, but not always to the point, the Constitution devotes 463 words to electing the president (46 percent) and 115 (20 percent) to appointments; thus, roughly two-thirds of Article II covers these two areas. "Power" is dealt with in roughly 20 percent of Article II. Why devote so much to Congress and so little to the executive? Perhaps because Congress was seen as, and empowered as, the key constitutional governing branch?

The inventors of the American executive office created a *republican presidency* of limited strength, possessing little independent power.[3] This reflects the ongoing fears of executive tyranny, sometimes referred to as tyrannophobia, harbored by the framers. But if the framers were so concerned with executive tyranny, why did they leave Article II so seemingly unfinished? Why not clearly and unmistakably stamp this new executive office as weak and small? There are two reasons for this: First, their initial effort at forming a government under the Articles of Confederation and Perpetual Union proved unworkable. Establishing a government with no executive office simply didn't work and couldn't work, and the framers soon recognized the fault in their reasoning. It is understandable that they might be so fearful of executive tyranny and so anti-executive that they would go to extremes, but operationally, not having some form of executive office proved a fatal flaw in their new system.

Second, when the framers were debating this new executive—this "president," an officer who would "preside"—their discussions took place in the shadow of the chair of the Constitutional Convention, George Washington. Washington was held in such high esteem by his countrymen that the men at the convention believed they could risk providing a skeletal version of the presidential office, trusting Washington to fill in the blanks and set the proper republican precedents.

This was an enormous risk, one commented on by Benjamin Franklin, who noted that he trusted Washington with this ill-defined office but held grave concerns regarding those who would follow Washington. Indeed, it was a risk, one strong-willed presidents would on occasion exploit.

How best then, to sculpt this new office for a new republic? Some, such as Alexander Hamilton, hoped to imbue the office with a measure of energy and independence while others, such as James Madison, stressed separation-of-power issues and constitutional limits on the presidency.

In the end, the framers created a circumscribed presidency, not a dominant institution; a republican presidency, not a monarchical office. The president would have few independent powers—most would be shared, but the office was imbued with enough power to hold its own in the tug-of-war that was the separation of powers. A model of concurrent authority and joint decision-making was created in the Constitution. Justice Robert Jackson was correct when he wrote that the Constitution "enjoins upon its branches not separateness but interdependence, not autonomy but reciprocity."[4]

Thus, we cannot understand the presidency unless we see it as connected to the other parts of government. Ours is a shared and overlapping model of power that requires some measure of consensus and cooperation for the other parts of government to run smoothly. This necessitates a government of consensus, coalition, and cooperation on the one hand and checks, vetoes, and balances on the other.

The key mechanisms the framers created to control and to empower the new executive include the following:

1. *Limited constitutional government* (a reaction against the arbitrary powers exercised by a king or state and also as a protection of personal liberty).
2. *Rule of law* (so that only on the basis of law could the government legitimately act).
3. *Separation of powers* (so that the three branches would each have a defined sphere of power).
4. *Checks and balances* (so that each branch could limit the powers of the other branches).

On its own, the presidency is a somewhat politically anemic institution. The framers did not make it easy for the government to act or for presidents to dominate. They left the powers and controls of the office somewhat vague and ambiguous. Looking at the framers' design, a modern efficiency expert would conclude that the system simply could not work: too many limits, too many checks; not enough power. No one was in charge. There is no authoritative focus of power.

A system of cross-powers and checked powers created a constitutional mechanism, designed to prevent one branch from exercising unilateral power. Opportunities to check power abound; opportunities to exercise power are limited. As Justice Louis Brandeis noted, "The doctrine of the separation of powers was adopted by the Convention of 1787, not to promote efficiency, but to preclude the exercise of arbitrary power. The purpose was not to avoid friction, but by means of the inevitable friction incident to the distribution of the governmental powers among three departments, to save the people from autocracy."[5]

This system of separation of powers and checks and balances was designated to prevent tyranny, not to promote efficiency. By these standards, it has worked well. At times, however, the lethargy built into the process threatens to grind the system to a halt. Yet it is a system that has largely escaped the crisis of executive tyranny. This fluidity and fragmentation of power created a situation in which "the government" is controlled not by any single person or institution but by different people in different places at different times, sometimes seeking different ends.

Often, today's debate over the framers' view of presidential power is couched as a Hamilton versus Jefferson debate, with Alexander Hamilton favoring a powerful presidency and Thomas Jefferson (who was not at the convention) advocating a weaker presidency. Such a simplistic distinction does violence to the views of both Hamilton *and* Jefferson.

Indeed, Hamilton did support an "energetic" executive, but he also—in the Federalist Papers (nos. 67–77)—supported the presidency as a "republican" office and as part of the separation-of-powers system. Weak executive advocates have also pointed to Thomas Jefferson, who, while calling for government closer to the people and a more limited presidency, nonetheless saw circumstances when the executive might be compelled to act, even at times beyond the strict limits of the law.

Making Sense of a Complex Institution

Because of the ambiguous nature of presidential power, both scholars and practitioners (presidents and their top staffers as well) have long attempted to solve the mystery of just what key unlocks the door to presidential power. The old joke is that there are three rules to being an effective president . . . the problem is no one knows what they are.

Presidents thus have limited power, yet the public has inflated expectations of what might be achieved. This almost always leads to disappointment in our presidents, as few can meet this "expectations gap." But having a president-centric executive has its costs. "As a president-obsessed nation, we undermine the very idea of our constitutional democracy by focusing so much on one person."[6]

We are very demanding of our presidents; we are impatient as well. Unfairly so? Probably. Perhaps an analogy will be useful here. In Olympic diving, the harder the attempted dive, the more credit or weight is given to the high degree of difficulty being attempted. Perhaps the hardest dive to nail is the reverse four-and-a-half somersault in the pike position. A diver who goes for this very difficult dive deserves more credit than another diver who perfectly executes a simple forward dive.

An example closer to home might be how to measure whether your professor's exam question was just too difficult to answer. Need proof? Calculate a question's "degree of difficulty" by taking the number of correct answers and dividing that number by the total number of students. If one hundred students take an exam and only ten got question no. 4 incorrect, the degree of difficulty on that question is "0.9," a fairly easy question. But if ninety of one hundred got it wrong, the question itself would have a high degree of difficulty. The fault may be more with the question being asked than with the students who got the answer wrong.

For presidents, the degree of difficulty is high even for many routine activities. Most of what a president is expected to do is hard. If a president faces a Congress controlled by the opposition party, his degree of difficulty will be in the 9 out of 10 range. If, on the other hand, the president's party controls both houses with large majorities, his degree of difficulty is much lower. In a crisis, Congress and the public demand presidential leadership. In this case, the degree of difficulty (in exercising power) is low.

The problem is presidents rarely have a low degree of difficulty. Not only do they face opposition to what they wish to do, but the problems they face are the most vexing problems imaginable. Easy problems are solved before they reach the president's desk. Thus, presidents are expected to solve the most difficult of problems with limited support or power. Degree of difficulty? Almost always very high.

There are essentially three approaches applied by presidency scholars that seek to explain how the presidency and presidential power can best be understood: the *power model*, the *persuasion model*, and the *paradox model*. Each approach highlights a different aspect of the presidency.

The *power model* posits that the president actually has considerable unilateral power. Scholars such as William G. Howell argue that "direct presidential action," that is, steps a president takes without Congress, on his own, composes a significant part of a president's arsenal.[7] Presidents need to better understand this power, exercise it more wisely, and command more and persuade less. Presidents do not have sufficient resources to persuade; but they do however have executive powers they may exercise.

The second model, the *persuasion model*, stresses not the president's independent powers but the office's dependency on others. In a *shared* system, presidents will often need the cooperation of others—especially Congress—if they are to accomplish their goals. Thus, persuasion, deal making, bargaining, and compromise are important tools of presidential success. Richard E. Neustadt's classic work *Presidential Power* is perhaps the most representative work in this area. Neustadt saw more weakness than power in the presidency, and so in order to govern, the president must "go Washington," develop significant "prestige" within the Beltway, and creatively apply his personal skills in trying to influence Congress to follow his lead.[8]

The third model, the *paradox model*, sees the presidency as a series of complex, contradictory, and paradoxical relationships and interactions in which the strategy that works for one president may not work for others. Additionally, the public has contradictory expectations and demands (e.g., we want a problem-solver in the White House, yet are so suspicious of centralized power that we fear a strong presidency; we want more services but lower taxes). Thus, gaining power means using a *leadership* approach to managing the office, where presidents must calculate power opportunities in each interaction, diagnose the problem, make a clear prescription, and apply it with skill, timing, and creativity.[9]

Which of these three models or approaches best explains and predicts presidential performance? That, of course, is a point of debate among presidency scholars. In the chapters that follow, you may see one model applying well in one case but not as well or of little use in another. You may see all three as having some utility depending on what is being examined. Are these three approaches really so different? Perhaps these models should be seen as a continuum rather than as discrete categories. Think of power at one end of our axis, persuasion anchoring the other end, with paradox in the middle (figure o.1).

These are all viable options from which a president may choose—depending on the president's skill repertoire, central tendencies, policy arena, and context. A strategic president

Power	Paradox	Persuasion
Howell	Cronin, Genovese, and Bose	Neustadt
Power Without Persuasion	*The Paradoxes of the American Presidency*	*Presidential Power*

FIGURE 0.1 The "Three Ps" approach to presidential leadership

assesses the terrain, decides on which approach is most likely to lead to success given the constraints and opportunities, devises a tactic to implement the strategy, and maintain hands-on implementation to (hopefully) bring policies to fruition.

Think of it as a coach in a basketball game who trains his team in one form of play (say, for example, stressing outside shooting and three-pointers), but in the actual game, if the opposing coach decides to extend his team's defense in an effort to offset the three-pointer, then our first coach, if he recognizes the opposing team's strategy, might call a time-out and readjust the team's strategy, emphasizing instead the inside game. Adaptability, discernment, diagnosis, and flexibility are the keys.

So too with presidents. A one-size-fits-all approach rarely works. Effective leaders style-flex (i.e., are adaptable), often trying to match their dance with the beat of the music being played. That is why I, among others, emphasize the paradox, or leadership, model. But you will see some presidents, such as Donald Trump, who employ a limited or even rigid power approach. Trump was a full speed ahead, go 95 mph even when approaching a dangerous hairpin turn type of president. He did not adapt to conditions; he demanded that everyone else adapt to him. This approach was well suited to the age of the divine right of kings but ill suited to the politics of a constitutional republic. Such presidents may do well from time to time (after all, a broken watch does tell the correct time twice a day), but overall, presidents who maintain a narrow range of approaches or styles tend to do poorly. Being flexible, adapting to different contexts, and accurately reading the circumstances is key to success. Just as individuals who have a high degree of emotional intelligence do better in life than those with lower levels, so too do presidents who have a high degree of executive intelligence and contextual intelligence do better than others.

But the question remains: Is one approach to the presidency of more utility than others in helping us understand the politics of the presidency? As the chapters in this book will suggest, the Sherlock Holmes problem-solving method may be of use.[10]

Sir Arthur Conan Doyle's master detective was a keen observer, was focused on available evidence, and was skilled at connecting the dots. When facing a particularly vexing case, he revealed one of the keys to his method of detection: "Once you eliminate the impossible, whatever remains, no matter how improbable, must be the truth."[11]

As you go about reading this book, and as contradictions and paradoxes litter our path, remember that amid confusion there are clues, bits of evidence that can guide us. Always, always follow the evidence, even when, especially when it conflicts with our preconceived notions. With that in mind, let us turn our attention to the American presidency to see how the institution operates and how the people who have occupied the office have attempted to grab power and govern.

It should be pointed out that few presidents make the presidency work effectively. That being the case, we must ask as: Is something fundamentally wrong with the presidency? Is the job too big for one person? Or do we just keep electing the wrong people? Is the office and its powers too difficult to manage? Is the separation of powers at the root of our problems of failed presidential leadership?

Management guru Peter Drucker gives us a straightforward way of evaluating this dilemma: "The rule is simple. Any job that has defeated two or three men in succession, even though each had performed well in his previous assignments, must be assumed unfit for human beings. It must be redesigned."[12]

At an earlier stage in my career (I've been teaching and writing about the presidency for more than forty years), I attempted

to understand and explain repeatedly disappointing presidencies by referring to what I called "America's Leadership Aver-
sion System."[13] In that analysis, while presidential skill levels
and decision-making were important, I argued that several
forces largely external to the president impeded effectiveness:
the intent of the framers (in trying to limit the executive from
becoming tyrannical); the structure of American government
(separation-of-powers system); our political culture (individu-
alistic and antigovernment); and the selection process (which
often rewards qualities we should avoid and punishes those who
possess the qualities we should seek). These forces put the presidents in a no-win situation unless faced with a crisis. Those factors still loom large and will be revisited throughout this book.

But in the intervening years, I have become more sensitive to
individual variations in skill and emotional intelligence, in levels
of political opportunity, and in context or circumstances. I have
also been informed by Niccolò Machiavelli, who in *The Prince*
discussed the three key elements of leadership as:

Virtù: By which he meant skill and judgment put into practice for the
good of the people, somewhat akin to what Aristotle meant
by *phronesis*.

Occasione: Context or circumstances. Different times called for and
allowed different types of opportunities. Some circumstances
called for boldness while others called for restraint. Effective
leaders knew when to turn up the pressure and when to back
away.

Fortuna: Luck. A leader could do all the right things yet fail if bad
luck intervened. For example, Jimmy Carter had the mis-
fortune of being president when the oil-producing nations
(OPEC) were unified and powerful and caused a global economic recession, while Ronald Reagan had the good fortune

to be president when OPEC was rapidly weakening, helping bring about an economic revival.

Virtù, occasione, fortuna. One needed all three to succeed. But this leadership trifecta rarely comes together. Thus, leaders were more often victims than masters of the situation. With this in mind I present my own version of the key ingredients necessary for presidential success:

THE PRESIDENTIAL SUCCESS MATRIX

For a president to "succeed" (to have power and to exercise it wisely), three forces must be in alignment:
1. Level of political opportunity

    Size of electoral victory, an issue-oriented campaign, majority of party in legislature, popularity, nature of political opposition, public demand for governmental action, issues in the congressional pipeline, etc.
2. Skill

    Experience, temperament, persuasive skills, managerial skills, cognitive abilities, communication, emotional intelligence, creativity, drive, empathy, judgment, self-assurance, situational intelligence, optimism, charisma, etc.
3. Context

    Separation of powers, domestic or foreign policy, crisis or normal times, deficit or surplus, level of trust in government, consensus or division, partisan makeup, global challenges, commitments, opportunities, etc.

In this book, we will try to answer the complex question: What must a president do in order to be successful? We will do this by examining six key questions or disputes that presidency scholars regularly confront in trying to get to the center of the problems posed by presidential leadership.

These discussions are drawn from the available academic literature and also reflect what we presidency scholars discuss and debate at conferences when we get together for drinks or dinner. Inevitably, the conversation is drawn into a usually friendly discussion of these issues, and they remain relevant because they remain unresolved and the source of debate.

Answering these questions will help us discern both the problems and possibilities of effective presidential leadership. The six key questions are as follows:

- What is more important, *power* or *persuasion?*
- What matters more, the *individual* or the *institution?*
- Did the framers invent a powerful *unitary executive* or a limited *constitutional office?*
- Which is more valuable, *character* or *competence?*
- What is more important, *skill* or *opportunity?*
- Will the future of the U.S. presidency be one of *liberal democracy* or *illiberal democracy?*

We will better understand what strengths and weaknesses presidents bring to the table; how the table is set and what that tells us of presidential power; how and why previous presidents succeeded and failed; the rules (or norms) that presidents are supposed to follow; the constitutional and political elements of the office; what past presidents did that worked and what they did that didn't work; and where to find—and use—the keys to unlocking presidential power.

1

WHAT IS MORE IMPORTANT, POWER OR PERSUASION?

If it's between good and bad, somebody else will deal with it. Everything that gets into the Oval Office is between bad and worse.

—Rahm Emanuel, chief of staff to Barack Obama

Of the many things about which presidency scholars disagree, the gulf between those who argue that power is the key to understanding presidential leadership versus those who see persuasion as the key is perhaps the most significant divide.

Why do presidency scholars fret so about this question? Because we've been trying for decades to figure out the secret sauce of presidential leadership. What actually produces success in our separated system of shared and overlapping powers?

Left to his own devices, is the president powerful or weak, Leviathan or Sisyphus? A president's inbox is always overflowing. Does he face these problems from a position of great strength or weakness?

Let's try to sort out this puzzle. Professor Smith walks into a U.S. foreign policy class and begins her lecture with: "The president has enormous power. He controls hundreds of nuclear weapons that can be launched on his orders, destroy virtually all life on the planet, commencing a nuclear war that would make the earth a wasteland." Professor Smith is correct in this analysis.

In your next class on U.S. domestic policy, Professor Brown opens her class lecture with: "The president is too weak. Dependent on others to accomplish his goals, the president can't even authorize a small tax cut without Congress giving its approval. And even then, the court can put a stop to it. Presidents are weak; they have very little power to act." Professor Brown is correct in her analysis.

But how can they both be right? Welcome to the *Goldilocks dilemma* in presidential leadership, where presidential power is simultaneously too hot and too cold. Too hot in war and foreign policy, too cold in domestic and economic policy. We can't seem to get it just right. Paradoxes, while disconcerting, quite often describe the office.

But why is the president a powerful Leviathan in foreign affairs but a frustrated Sisyphus in domestic policy?

Leviathan is a biblical sea monster. It is also the title of Thomas Hobbes's 1651 classic of political philosophy in which Hobbes argued that the battle against violence and chaos of the political world, where life is "nasty, brutish, and short," means that the country needed a powerful, even absolute monarch who, with the consent of the governed, imposed order and stability.

In some ways, the international political scene is chaotic and a place where power usually determines outcome, a world Hobbes would recognize. In such a world, a strong leader may be seen as beneficial, maybe even necessary. In the United States, the presidency is supposed to fill this role. And in that role, the president is granted considerable power to fulfill the expectation.

In foreign affairs, the president exercises powers that are significant, but in the domestic arena, the president is hemmed in by an assertive Congress, a demanding public, an occasionally influential judiciary, and various interest groups. The president's domestic and economic authority is thus quite limited. Too hot abroad, too cold at home.

The domestic arena often presents the president as Sisyphus, doomed to forever roll a boulder up a hill, only to have it roll back down as he approaches the top.

In foreign affairs, the presidential Leviathan can often rely on power; in domestic affairs, the presidential Sisyphus must work hard to persuade others to support his efforts.

THE PROBLEM CLEARLY STATED

What is the president's source of strength? Does the president have sufficient *power* to act or must he lead and try to *persuade* others to follow? Power versus persuasion, which moves the system?

WHY IT MATTERS

If a president is to succeed, he must efficiently and wisely move the pieces across the political chessboard in ways that are both timely and authoritative. What are the key resources at his disposal, and which are most likely to unlock the doors to power?

The power/persuasion argument is a part of the command or leadership elements of the presidency. Yes, presidents have some power, but just how much? And yes, presidents must seek to persuade, but is that all they've got?

In a constitutional republic, presidents are bound by the rule of law and the separation of power. He is but one part of a three-institution system. How much raw power can he exercise, and how often must he do the hard work of convincing and coalition building?

The Constitution gives us some guidance. It gives each branch some power but, for the most part, sets up a sharing and intermingling of power. The president has few independent or plenary powers. He is well positioned to lead but has limited authority to command. The result? Presidents are often seen as failing to meet expectations. But do we give the president the tools to be successful?

POWER

We often assume that the president has "power." After all, he is the focus of media attention, and we see the drama of American politics as a story of presidential politics. Presidents get vastly more attention than does Congress, giving us the (mis)impression that the president *is* the government. But ours is a story of three branches, not one, and one cannot truly understand American politics by focusing *only* on the presidency.

The media attention lavished upon the presidency may lead us to mistakenly believe that the president has more power than he does. Then, when things go wrong, we blame the president, and when things go well, we praise the president. But our shared system of power necessitates some cooperation and consensus, lest things break down. That they so often break down is inherent in a constitutional republic with a separation of powers.

Congress is slow moving. Its sclerotic system is often moribund, difficult to move through. By contrast, the presidency is built for speed; it is a streamlined institution.

The separation-of-powers system often makes Congress a place of no return for a president's legislative agenda. Must a president merely accept congressional intransigence? If Congress continues to fiddle while Main Street burns, is a president helpless? Meeting with considerable congressional lethargy, some presidents will find end runs around Congress. Executive action is sometimes an option for the president.

If you want to understand how political power is imposed, read Robert Caro's extraordinary 1975 book, *The Power Broker: Robert Moses and the Fall of New York*. Caro demonstrates how raw power can get things done. He also demonstrates the high cost and risks of such power.[1]

The late Anthony King highlighted institutional characteristics that help us identify those executives who possesses "power." King defines power as "power—or influence, or strength . . . that the head of government can exercise *within his or her own governmental system*. The question will be: To what extent is the head of government in a position to assert his or her will over the rest of the cabinet, the civil service, and the national legislature?"[2]

King then examines the key factors that indicate the executive truly has power. These factors are as follows:

1. *Terms of the Constitution*. How much "power" is constitutionally conferred to the executive?
2. *Direct elections by the people*. Who chooses the executive, the party, the legislature, or the people?
3. *Security of tenure*. How vulnerable is the executive to within-term removal?
4. *Effective leader of political party*. Is the executive in charge of his or her party?
5. *Control of or influence within the legislature*. Is the legislature "independent" of the executive?

6. *Control of appointments.* Does the executive have the power to create or eliminate government agencies?

7. *Structure of the executive board.* Does the executive have the hierarchical authority within his or her government?

8. *Control of the civil service.* Is the executive in command of the civil service system or is it independent of a president's control?

9. *Public prestige.* To King, public support matters.

10. *Staff size.* Is the executive branch or president's team fully staffed to give the executive adequate support?

Taken together, the American presidency is only a marginally powerful institution. Presidents register low or fairly low on King's numbers 1, 2, 5, 7, and 8; high on 3, 4, 6, 9, and 10. Compared to the leaders of the other advanced industrial democracies, the American president ranks in the middle of the pack on "power."

What of persuasion? Richard Neustadt's 1960 book, *Presidential Power*,[3] became the dominant paradigm for presidential scholars and remained central to the study of the presidency for sixty years. When I was in graduate school in the late 1970s, it was taken for granted that Neustadt's definition of presidential power as "the power to persuade" was true. There were alternative views, but they existed at the margins of presidential studies.

But in the early 2000s, cracks began to appear in the Neustadt paradigm. Works by Kenneth Mayer on executive orders, Phillip Cooper on "direct administration" by a president, and Greg Robinson on FDR's direct action challenged the persuasion orthodoxy and focused attention on direct presidential action.[4] In addition, scholars who employed rational choice theory, such as Charles Cameron and Patricia Conley,[5] introduced game theory and other approaches to understanding a president's strategic environment.

Some policies were being set and implemented *without Congress*. Direct unilateral action in the form of executive orders, administrative directives, executive memoranda, and proclamations give the president a means to "go it alone." Of course, presidents have always used these tools, sometimes to implement significant new public policies (e.g., FDR unilaterally ordered the internment of more than 110,000 Japanese Americans in World War II, and Harry Truman used executive authority to desegregate the military). Increasingly in a political environment characterized by hyperpartisanship and divided government, presidents often found direct action as the preferable, perhaps only way to change policies.

The president has the unique advantage of being in the strategic position to move first and act alone.[6] The president can initiate action on his own, then see if Congress balks. If so, he may be in a battle, but the stage is already set for the achievement of his policy. If not, then game, set, and match. If the courts get involved, it is usually late in the game, and if they decide to limit a presidential act, the president might accept that decision, slow walk the policy back, or make readjustments and go ahead with a slightly different policy.

Some political scientists have attempted to marry power and persuasion, offering a more political or strategic version of the presidency.[7] This view sees a president trying to diagnose context so as to discern what approach to take. Here, power might work; elsewhere, persuasion might seem the best course.[8]

Long story short, there is a great deal that presidents *can do on their own* and *without Congress*. They need not always rely on persuasion or permission.

PERSUASION

Yes, while presidents do have some room to act unilaterally, for significant and lasting change, acting alone may be insufficient. To make big changes, have them stick, and make them hard to undo, *presidents need Congress to pass laws.*[9]

Landmark legislation remains the gold standard: President Obama's ACA (Health Care Act) and President Biden's COVID stimulus package represent major new laws that mattered. And to pass landmark legislation, a president needs to persuade Congress to support his initiatives. Such persuasion is considerably easier when the president has a large working majority of his party in control of both houses of Congress, but even then, presidents usually have to do a considerable amount of leveraging, deal making, and bargaining in order to get what they want.

In the Madisonian system created by the founders, three branches shared power while also maintaining quasi-independent sources of power so as to defend themselves against encroachment by the other branches. Power was to counteract power, ambition counteract ambition. A separation of powers and checks and balances meant interaction and collaboration were necessary to get the Goldilocks dilemma "just right."

The founders did not make it easy for the government to act or the president to lead, but again efficiency was not the goal; the prevention of tyranny and promotion of liberty were the goals. To elicit the best out of this system of separate, shared, and overlapping powers, presidents had to build coalitions, generate consensus, bargain, pressure, make deals, compromise, push and pull. In short, they had to persuade. Neustadt was clearly onto something.

The executive was to have "energy," to use Hamilton's term from Federalist no. 70, but it was energy of a republican variety, not unilateral, independent energy, or at least not very much of that. Presidents, if they were to get legislation passed, had to bring into synchronization that which the founders separated.

This requires political appeal. It requires persuasion. Of course, not all policy change requires legislation, and yes presidents do have and do exercise a modicum of direct unilateral authority. A president who doesn't or can't persuade may feel compelled to rely on direct presidential action, but an executive order by one president can be—and often is—undone by his successor. President Trump undid many of President Obama's orders, and President Biden did the same to President Trump's.

A STORY

Presidents—especially as candidates—make promises. The public tends to take these promises with a grain of salt. We are cynical about our politicians, and while hope may spring eternal, a measure of caution, if not distrust, is pervasive in American politics.

That said, it might surprise citizens that in general, politicians take their promises/commitments very seriously.[10] Study after study reveals that officeholders go to great lengths to keep as many of their promises as possible, and even given the understandable roadblocks built into our separation-of-powers system, politicians are willing to invest a great deal of time, effort, and political capital in attempting to deliver on their promises.[11]

Candidate Barack Obama, both because he believed in the justice of helping undocumented children in the United States, and because Hispanic voters were an important voting bloc for the Democrats, gave his commitment that, if elected president, he would do all he could to protect and help undocumented minors in the United States. And try he did—but not right away.

Obama, as a new president, had other items on his wish list that were deemed more important than the plight of undocumented children. Presidents can't do everything at once. They must prioritize their agendas, and for Obama, year one would focus on the passage of comprehensive health care. In year two, jobs and other issues rose to the top of the agenda.

Disgruntled Hispanics pressed the administration to fulfill Obama's campaign promise, and eventually, Obama asked Congress to pass a law protecting undocumented children. The DREAM Act, an effort to grant legal status to young immigrants living in the United States, stalled in Congress. First considered in 2007 in the last year of the George W. Bush presidency, the bill failed to gain the Senate's approval. In 2011, the bill was reintroduced where it passed the House but was stalled in the Senate.

Pressed to act by key Democrats, Obama eventually felt compelled to eschew the legislative route and in 2012 issued a memorandum (technically from the secretary of Homeland Security) entitled "Exercising Prosecutorial Discretion with Respect to Individuals Who Came to the United States as Children"); the new executive policy allowed certain immigrants to escape deportation and receive work permits.[12]

Republicans balked. This, many claimed, was an "abuse of power," and in 2013, all House Republicans and three Democrats voted to defund DACA. Several lawsuits were filed claiming, among other things, that President Obama exceeded his authority by unilaterally "making law." The Supreme Court, in 2020, upheld the legality of Obama's DACA policy.

President Obama was unable to persuade Congress to pass DACA legislation, so he imposed it via executive authority. Was this an example of "executive overreach" or a legitimate exercise of the president's executive authority? That question is open to interpretation, but it is also an example of what president's do when they fail to persuade Congress to approve their proposals. The fallback executive action approach may not be ideal—clearly Obama would have preferred establishing DACA guarantees via a new law—but when all else fails, and it usually does, presidents may see executive acts as their only remaining option.[13]

In skating on thin ice, the president risks seeing his executive action undone by a successor's executive action, and a merry-go-round effect of one party asserting executive authority only to be reversed by the next administration begins. The candidate of the rival party becomes president and undoes his predecessor's executive action with executive action of his own, then the first president's party returns to power only to reimpose the executive action of the first president. In short, executive action can be temporary and open to reversal.

Persuasion thus has its limits. But so too does power. The genius, or the frustration, of the American system is that in a separated system, presidents must diagnose the situation, estimate which approach to take, then apply that approach with skill and even guile. Power *or* persuasion? More like power *and* persuasion.

MY VIEW

Leadership is not linear; it is not the result of a clear road map that points the way. It is octagonal, many sided, a multidimensional puzzle; it *is* rocket science.

To me, the power/persuasion argument misses the point. It is not an either/or case. Power and persuasion are both essential elements of a president's arsenal. A strategically adept president uses both. At times, the power approach is appropriate; at other times, persuasion is the key. A president must survey the political landscape, diagnose the problem, then apply the appropriate remedy or strategy to fix the problem.

A useful way to understand the power versus persuasion argument is to borrow a concept from international relations. Harvard's Joseph Nye Jr. has written extensively about the differences between hard and soft power. By hard power, Nye means coercive power, force, military might, and economic advantages. It is the ability to compel others to obey or concede. According to Nye, it is "the ability to use carrots and sticks of economic and military might to make others follow your will."[14]

Soft power is the ability to attract others to your position. This may be a function of others admiring you or wishing to emulate you or, where others look up to us, want to be more like us, do as we do, behave as we behave. Soft power is, to quote Nye, a function of "credibility," or "where one country gets other countries to want what it wants might be called co-optive or soft power in contrast with the hard or command power of ordering others to do what it wants."[15]

As you've already surmised, what one refers to as *persuasion* is a version of *soft power*, while *power* is a form of *hard power*. Soft power was, to Neustadt, about reputation and prestige. And presidents may also exercise hard power when they can command others and expect others to comply.

Smart power might be conceived of as the ability to strategically devise means to achieve one's aims by recognizing when and how to apply soft or hard power, depending on the circumstances. Effective presidents apply smart power to problems faced.

I do not believe we should treat this as an either/or debate. These two approaches to governing are complementary and not necessarily contradictory, and effective presidents will assess the political territory to determine which of these approaches best fits a president's needs of the moment. And the nature of the achieved changes must from time to time be revisited, necessitating a reevaluation and perhaps new diagnosis as well as a new prescription. A president locked in either to a power or persuasion model will unnecessarily self-limit.

Strategic presidents are able to assess the situation and apply the appropriate style that is most likely to lead to success. He looks before he leaps. On one issue, pursue a legislative remedy; on another, go it alone. Power *and* persuasion.

CONCLUSION

A test of presidential effectiveness (or skill) is the ability to diagnose, prescribe, apply, and execute one's agenda given the circumstances faced. A one-size-fits-all approach (persuasion or power) will usually yield sparse results. Presidents must be flexible, adaptable, and quick on their feet.

2

WHAT MATTERS MORE, THE INDIVIDUAL OR THE INSTITUTION?

t was late August 1973, my first day of graduate school at the University of Southern California. The professor in my very first graduate class was James Rosenau, one of the superstars in the field of international relations and a charismatic teacher. He opened the first class with a question: "Do leaders matter?" As one might expect, the question was met with silence. Who wanted to take the risk of being first to speak and, perhaps, the first person whom the professor could use as an example of just how dumb we all were?

The question seemed so simple, so easy, a softball that our kindly professor tossed up, giving us an opportunity to shine and hit the first pitch out of the park. And yet, no one spoke. We suspected a trap.

As you've probably already guessed, I, with more courage than brains, took a shot: "Of course," I said, "leaders matter." A sly smile crossed Professor Rosenau's face. I knew I was in trouble. "Why?" he asked. After all these years, I do not remember much about my answer, except that Rosenau removed a stiletto from his coat and proceeded to slice and dice me up and down and side to side. I didn't give up, I didn't give in (much), until I finally said, "Okay, you win round one, but if we can revisit this question at the end of the semester, I'll be better able to take on this question."

We never revisited the question in class, but that question, so simple, yet so complex, came to define a central point in my chosen field of study, the presidency.

Yes—I would still argue—leaders and presidents matter, but not always, and not always in ways we might think. And it is that question to which we now turn: Do presidents matter?

AND NOW FOR SOMETHING COMPLETELY DIFFERENT

In the immediate aftermath of the 2016 presidential election, a number of commentators expressed fears that Donald Trump, a political outsider and self-proclaimed "disruptor" who promised radical change and a series of unorthodox policies (e.g., locking up his electoral rival Hillary Clinton, building a wall at the southern border that Mexico would be paying for, banning *all* Muslims from entering the United States), would so disrupt the status quo that chaos might ensue. Don't worry, others said, the presidency would soon tame Mr. Trump.

It turned out that the presidency *did not* tame Trump, it revealed him and gave him the opportunity to impose his personality, policies, and operating style onto the institution. True, the courts and at times Congress stood in Trump's way, and the press proved a thorn in his side, but within the executive branch, Trump called the shots and employed a strategy of bullying, firings, sending out (sometimes vulgar) tweet attacks, and simply refusing to rely on the wisdom of experienced hands or on available evidence in making decisions. The White House was his sandbox, and he forced everyone in it to play by *his* rules.[1]

I will grant you, Donald Trump may be an extreme example, an outlier whose "my way or the highway" style that he adapted from the business world became his operating style as president, but is Trump really the exception? He may be the most obvious example of the man shaping the institution, but is he alone?

THE PROBLEM CLEARLY STATED

The president is an individual, the presidency is an institution. The president is a single person, the presidency is a large collection of people, organizations, and agencies. Each influences the other. The individual must rely on the institution for information, advice, assistance, and implementation. The institution must respond to the individual but can also coax or point the president in a particular direction. The individual has his own needs political and otherwise, the institution its own requirements The president tends to think short-term (I need it "now"), the bureaucracy is in no big rush. They coexist. The individual is there for a few years. The institution is ongoing. Which matters most, under which conditions? Is the president stronger than the institution or vice versa?

WHY DOES THIS MATTER?

If the individual is dominant, ways must be found to make the institution effectively serve his needs, while also channeling presidential behavior in appropriate directions. If the institution drives the individual, ways must be found to make the layers of government more professional and efficient, as well as more responsive to the needs and demands of the democratically elected president and the interests of the American people.

DO LEADERS MATTER?

Many, perhaps most, scholars in the field of international relations are skeptical regarding the role the individual plays in shaping change. Such scholars see structural, institutional, international, and national-interest elements driving policy. Leaders—those in a position to make decisions—are more hemmed in by roles and expectations, prior commitments, resources, and circumstances than by the whims, will, or goals of the individual (figure 2.1).

This debate goes back many years. After all, the great thinkers from Plato to Aristotle and Machiavelli to Marx all weighed in on the role and importance of individual leadership in guiding the polity or the state. In the 1800s, British historian Thomas Carlyle, in his book *On Heroes, Hero-Worship, and the Heroic in History*, argued that history is made by great men imposing their wills over events. As Carlyle has written, "The history of the world is but the biography of great men."[2] Great men make things happen. Napoleon changed Europe. Jesus changed religion. Hitler caused World War II, Caesar crossed the Rubicon, FDR ended the Great Depression and won World War II, Lincoln freed the slaves, and Newton discovered gravity.

There is no doubt that these consequential leaders mattered. But where would Jesus Christ be were it not for the apostles, both writing the Bible and propagating the faith? Jesus spoke

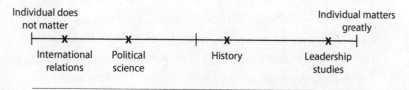

FIGURE 2.1 Academic fields and their positions on the role of individuals in change

the words, the apostles spread the Word. Christ needed followers. Without them, he would have been merely another religious preacher in search of a flock.

Person, situation, capacity: Agency requires all three, and the *great man theory* posits that great men acting greatly bend the arc of history. Some presidency scholars advance this view either implicitly or explicitly. Lyndon Johnson is responsible for the Civil Rights and Voting Rights Acts of the 1960s, Ronald Reagan ended the Cold War, George H. W. Bush won the First Gulf War, and his son lost the second one.

By contrast, others believed that the great man theory was naïve and that leaders were more the products of their environment than masters of them, and that the drawing power of the great man theory stems from the fact that it is comprehensible, simple, and easy to accept.[3]

Russian novelist Leo Tolstoy strongly disagreed with Carlyle. In his classic novel *War and Peace* (1869), Tolstoy argues that leaders are products of their times, not creators of them. Tolstoy argues that Napoleon was the product and beneficiary of his time, and while we focus on Napoleon's leadership, decisions, and strategic moves, in focusing on one man we neglect a rich variety of other factors that shaped the situation. Yes, Napoleon barked out orders, but how many were followed, how many ignored, and how many never even got to his commanders in the field? And as the battle was waged, Napoleon could only—at best—have a very limited knowledge of events at the front or at multiple fronts. *Fortuna*, as Machiavelli reminds us, can determine results.[4]

Did the English at Agincourt, outnumbered three or four to one, really rally to the inspiring words of Henry V (as handed down to us by Shakespeare) or was it the fact the English discovered that the ewe tree could be made into a long bow, thereby allowing English archers to kill French troops before they even

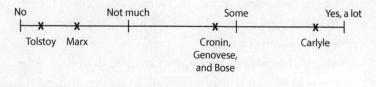

FIGURE 2.2 Leading views: Do leaders matter?

got a chance to engage the English in battle? Which gave them the upper hand, leadership or technology?

Nico Mouton's analysis of Tolstoy and critics of the great man theory concludes: "The Great Man Theory presents leaders as powerful geniuses, capable of producing comprehensive plans that foresee all contingencies, and of controlling enormously complex concerted actions. Tolstoy constructs a counter-narrative that portrays leaders as vain ignoramuses, their power as an illusion, their plans as irrelevant, and their orders as ineffectual."[5] And Karl Marx reminds us that "men make their own history, but they do not make it as they please; they do not make it under self-selected circumstances, but under circumstances existing already, given and transmitted from the past."[6]

Is it either/or, or is it a balance and interaction of factors? Do leaders matter sometimes, in some ways, in some situations? As with most things, life is lived only very rarely at the extremes (figure 2.2). We now turn our attention to the individual and/or the institution.

INDIVIDUAL OR INSTITUTION?

The president is a person; the presidency is an institution. Which matters more, the man or the machine? Does the individual rule over, command, and dictate to the presidency or does the institution shape the occupant of the White House? True, this is not necessarily an either/or question, but the individual-versus-institution question serves to highlight, yet again, the paradoxical nature of the presidency. We tend to see the presidency as the president. This makes some superficial sense, for as journalist John Dickerson reminds us, "From the start, the office of the presidency was imbued with the behavior of its occupant."[7] In some very clear ways, the person *makes* the institution. But the institution also makes the man.

Questions of *agency* (is person X truly responsible for making change Y happen) and *causation* (the capacity of a person to have an impact on outcomes and whether he or she is truly the cause of the change) are always difficult to determine with certainty.

Institutions are settings in which presidents operate. At times, the best-laid plans of mice and men end in disaster when the best of ideas meet bureaucratic or managerial blunders.

A president appoints roughly four thousand people to executive branch jobs. Most will never see or work directly with the president. The bureaucratic mandarins run the day-to-day operations of the executive branch. They matter, but they generally do not "decide."

The staff and chief of staff are there to assist and serve the president. They are not—or should not be—the center of attention. This was emphasized in the 1930s Brownlow Report, which called for staffers who had "a passion for anonymity."[8] But a chief of staff can help organize a presidency and assist the president by managing the executive branch, bringing options and information to the president.

One could trace most presidential blunders to managerial or administrative errors. In the Bay of Pigs fiasco (1961), President Kennedy relied on bad information fed to him by the CIA and reinforced by inexperienced advisers around him. Yes, he made the decision to greenlight the operation, but his decision was a product of a bureaucratic mess-up.

Watergate was a result of decisions made by President Nixon and his team, but again, mismanagement sent events spiraling out of control. Where was the flashing red-light warning that crimes were just ahead? Where was the man or woman of integrity who would say no? (It took Attorney General Elliot Richardson to refuse to fire special prosecutor Archibald Cox in the Saturday Night Massacre to finally arrive at a person of honor.)

The list could go on and on: the war in Vietnam, the Iran-Contra scandal, the Second Gulf War, the early federal response to Hurricane Katrina and to the COVID-19 pandemic.[9] Bureaucratic and managerial blunders poisoned the policy well and led to disasters.

The greater the coordination and complementary qualities of an administration, the greater the likelihood of success, as "a presidency, like any large organization, requires coordinated action by extremely well-chosen teams."[10]

"Who" a president appoints can be just as important as "what" he wants to accomplish, as one leads to the other. And presidents reveal a great deal about themselves in the people they appoint to high positions. Historian Richard Norton Smith once said that "every president reveals himself by the presidential portraits he hangs in the Roosevelt Room, and by the person he picks as his Chief of Staff."[11]

Perhaps the most important quality a leader can have is *good judgment*. Problems that can be solved are usually handled below the presidential level. Only the most vexing of problems land on a president's desk. Thus, the president is responsible only for the most complex and wicked of problems.

Presidential decision-making has both an individual and an institutional component. At the individual level, presidents must confront complex problems and choose. What is the best way to deal with Kim Jong-un of North Korea? How can we handle the ravages of global climate change? Free trade, protectionism, or trade wars? What should we do about income inequality, the partisan wars in politics, race relations?

In making complex decisions, presidents rely on their knowledge of issues, party commitments, their experience, the information they are given, calculations of what is politically possible, expert analysis, and electoral imperatives, among other things. Individual presidents are also prone to the decision-making biases we all face, factors that inhibit good judgment and decision-making.

John F. Kennedy, reflecting on the complexity, not to mention mystery, of the act of decision-making noted that "the secret of the presidential enterprise is to be found in an examination of the way presidential choices are made. . . . The essence of ultimate decision remains impenetrable to the observer—often, indeed, to the decider himself."[12]

Smart, experienced leaders sometimes make inexcusable blunders, glaring mistakes that are clearly ill-advised and avoidable. Presidents, like the rest of us, are often led astray by common biases that infect our decision-making process. Biases such as *confirmation bias* (where we give greater value to information that supports our existing beliefs), *anchoring bias* (where we overly rely on early information), *overconfidence* (where we think too highly of our abilities), or *availability bias* (when we gravitate to information at our hands), and other biases all work to inhibit sound judgment.[13]

To illustrate, please answer the following question: How many of each animal did Moses take onto the ark? Almost everyone answers, two. But, of course, the answer is that Moses did not lead the animals onto the ark, Noah did. You knew that, so why did you come to such a dumb conclusion? Not because you are dumb, but because we have a habit of rushing to judgment without careful or deliberate thinking? The lesson here is that we cannot rely solely on our own judgment; we are too prone to biases, we need help.

Who is to help a president? A president's team. The cabinet and staff serve the president and provide ideas, information, and advice designed to help the president confront wicked problems. The president sits atop the most comprehensive information-gathering machine ever invented. But having information is one thing, having the right information presented in the right way at the right time with the right analysis is a different thing. Does a key staff member present to the president materials that support the staffer's preferred option? Did key bits of information fall through the cracks or somehow fail to reach the president's desk? Were key options excluded because of groupthink, where the pressure on staff to be team players ends up excluding important ideas that the majority does not advocate? Did the staff vet the issue fully? Consult key members of Congress? Core constituencies? Experts?

While the president's team is intent on assisting the president, the team may end up isolating him.[14] Historian Barbara W. Tuchman sees sheer "wooden-headedness"—as she puts it: "Assessing a situation in terms of preconceived and fixed notions while ignoring or rejecting any contrary signs," or "acting according to wish while not allowing oneself to be deflected by the facts,"[15]—as a source of folly both for individual leaders and their advisers. Ideology sometimes trumps evidence in decision-making. To Tuchman, "the rejection of reason is the prime characteristic of folly."[16]

Thus, we can see that both the individual (the president) and the institution (the presidency) are prone to decision-making errors. And good judgment encompasses more than just the president's ability to make sound decisions. A president and a team are required to make the machinery of the executive branch function effectively. A cognitively ill-equipped president, a dysfunctional team, or a flawed process can all produce corrupted or unsound decisions. The president and the team must work in syncopation to consistently produce constructive results. And even here—as Machiavelli reminds us—*fortuna* may work against the best-laid plans of teams and presidents.

Even presidential successes can be undone by poor execution. President Obama's Affordable Care Act (Obamacare) was his signature legislative victory. But implementation blunders in the program's rollout set the policy back a year or more. Likewise, President Trump's push to produce a vaccine for the COVID-19 virus produced vaccines in record time. But lack of a viable plan to distribute the vaccine led to thousands of unnecessary deaths.

Yes, leadership matters, but so does management. Effective presidents do the right things and do them well. When good ideas meet bad implementation, it is a particularly disappointing failure. We often know what to do, we just didn't know how to do it.

A STORY

Most people presume that the president is the presidency. But of course, the president is an individual while the presidency is an institution. Both contribute to executive branch outcomes. At times, they work together as a team; at other times, they conflict and cause problems. And when presidents have problems, the nation suffers.[17]

A case in point is the incessant conflict, finger-pointing, and blame-shifting that occurred in the final year of the Trump presidency relating to the administration's problem-ridden response to the outbreak of the COVID-19 crisis.[18]

When Donald Trump was running for the presidency in 2016, critics expressed concern that Trump's flamboyance, his "my way or the highway" approach, his disrupting style, and his "I know more than the experts" beliefs would cause friction if not internecine warfare in the administration. Trump's defenders responded that this was not a major concern as "the presidency would tame Trump." Who was right? Did Trump change the presidency or did the presidency change Trump? To explore this question, we can examine one of the most important challenges faced by the Trump administration: the COVID-19 crisis. In attempting to meet the challenge of the pandemic and the economic recession it caused, the administration went through three distinct phases: first, the initial response; second, the hunt for a vaccine; and finally, the vaccine distribution effort.[19]

In phase 1, when the virus first came to the government's attention (January 2020), the president was beginning his reelection bid. His goal was to downplay the severity of the virus, keep the economy open, not disrupt citizens' lives, and most of all present a "good news" version of reality on which to run for reelection. The problem was, things were not good, the pandemic was a fast-spreading, deadly disease that could kill hundreds of thousands of Americans—and the president knew it. Jeff Tollefson, in the journal *Nature*, sums up Trump's phase 1 response:

> The president of the United States has lied about the dangers posed by the coronavirus and undermined efforts to contain it; he even admitted in an interview to purposefully misrepresenting

the viral threat early in the pandemic. Trump has belittled masks and social-distancing requirements while encouraging people to protest against lockdown rules aimed at stopping disease transmission. His administration has undermined, suppressed, and censored government scientists working to study the virus and reduce its harm. And his appointees have made political tools out of the US Centers for Disease Control and Prevention (CDC) and the Food and Drug Administration (FDA), ordering the agencies to put out inaccurate information, issue ill-advised health guidance, and tout unproven and potentially harmful treatments for Covid-19.[20]

But inside the Trump administration, his COVID team was telling a different story than Trump. They tried to warn Trump that his rosy picture was wrong and dangerous. Two of his most prominent scientific advisors, Dr. Anthony Fauci, director of the U.S. National Institute of Allergy and Infectious Diseases, and Dr. Deborah Birx, the White House Coronavirus Response coordinator, repeatedly tried to warn Trump, even going so far as to publicly suggest that the president was wrong in his understanding of the severity of the disease.[21]

The irony here is that President Trump knew he was lying. As he told journalist Bob Woodward in the early days of the pandemic, the COVID-19 virus was "more deadly than even your strenuous flu." Yet, in public, the president kept dismissing the threat of virus as a minor annoyance that was "under control."

Woodward concluded: "A president must be willing to share the worst with the people, the bad news with the good. All presidents have a large obligation to inform, warn, protect, to define goals and the true national interest. It should be a truth-telling response to the world, especially in crisis. Trump has, instead, enshrined personal impulse as a governing principle of his presidency." And he added that President Trump's influence was the cause of problems:

> But now, I've come to the conclusion that the "dynamite behind the door" was in plain sight. It was Trump himself. The oversized personality. The failure to organize. The lack of discipline. The lack of trust in others he had picked, in experts. The undermining or the attempted undermining of so many American institutions. The failure to be a calming, healing voice. The unwillingness to acknowledge error. The failure to do his homework. To extend the olive branch. To listen carefully to others.[22]

In phase 2, President Trump's actions had a positive impact. While publicly trying to downplay the danger of the virus, Trump privately acknowledged the danger and directed that more than $13 billion go to private businesses to develop a vaccine for the virus. Ordinarily it takes well over a year to develop, test, and approve a new vaccine. But in Operation Warp Speed, Trump pressed pharmaceutical companies and government watchdog agencies to speed up the process. It worked. Less than a year after the start of the virus's spread, several vaccines were available for distribution.

And that brings us to phase 3, and another disaster by the Trump team. Developing the vaccine was a truly impressive task, but once developed, the vaccines had to be distributed, and plans had to be developed to get these vaccines into the arms of Americans. Here too, the administration failed. It had no implementation plan. When the Biden team came into office, its members realized they had vaccines but no mechanism for distribution. Why? How? It was so basic, so fundamental a goal, yet the Trump team utterly failed in its job, and the president, fresh off a loss in the 2020 election, gave up.[23]

Trump's battle against his own administration was revealed by the president himself when he said: "Based on their interviews [Fauci and Birx], I felt it was time to speak up about Dr. Fauci and Dr. Birx, two self-promoters trying to reinvent history to cover for their bad instincts and faulty recommendations which I fortunately almost always overturned."[24]

Is this any way to speak of your team? Not only does it devalue them, it also sends a message that the boss does not have your back. It suggests an administration at odds with itself, a dysfunctional team, and one that could not possibly govern effectively.

As the internal battles of Team Trump became a daily public spectacle, it became clear that the Trump administration was pursuing two different and largely incompatible goals: The health professionals were battling a deadly pandemic; Donald Trump was fighting a reelection battle.

There is no way to eliminate all impediments to sound decision-making, but there are things presidents can do to increase the likelihood that they will make sound decisions. Process is one key to effective decision-making. Presidents must establish a rational process that helps provide evidence and information, presents several sides of arguments, and offers the president a variety of options designed to give the president what he needs to decide. Process is no panacea, but when a president is provided with proper tools for deciding, we make it easier for that president to make choices on the basis of sound information.

Decision-making maladies can be diminished if the president is an astute manager of people and process. But presidents are notoriously bad managers, or more likely, refuse to spend precious time or political capital on managing. But to ignore management is to invite trouble.

In recent years we have witnessed the rise of the "anti-analytical presidency," defined as an administration that embraces a personalistic office where information and data are subordinated to the demands or needs of the individual president, and where rigorous science and robust information accumulation are secondary to the ideological or personal views of the president. Rather than rely on evidence, information, or data, rather than consult experts and scientists, an anti-evidence and anti-science bias has sometimes been employed in making policy, one that eschews critical thinking and turns a blind eye to the demands of logical reasoning. From the Trump administration's embrace of "alternative facts" to its anti-science approach to climate change, the refusal to rely on expertise and evidence became a central component of decision-making in the Trump inner circle.[25]

President Trump is known for personalizing process. In fact, he eschews "process." He believed he didn't need to read reports as he was already a "stable genius." Where past presidents met at the start of every day with a reading of the President's Daily Briefing (PDB), a compendium put together by the intelligence agencies of the key issues and challenges ahead, President Trump found the PDBs long and boring and often bypassed the briefings. Compounding the problem, Trump often expressed a distrust of the intelligence community over which he presided and refused to rely on the information provided by the intelligence professionals.

President Trump was warned numerous times as early as January 2020 that a lethal virus was spreading in Wuhan, China, and could cause a global pandemic. He dismissed or downplayed the seriousness of the coronavirus, thereby refusing to take sufficient early action that could have made a difference. Weeks were wasted, time when the United States could have put a testing, tracing, and isolation program in place, set social distancing and mask-wearing guidelines, and accumulated the necessary personal protective equipment (PPE) and ventilators.

The "process" got the warnings to the president. The president refused to listen.

An anti-analytical presidency has consequences,[26] often leading to faulty, incomplete, or misleading information. The tools for making sound decisions are available, and while no panacea, they can be effectively employed to heighten the odds in decision-making. Not to rely on them is a choice presidents sometimes make, often with tragic consequences. We cannot force a president to seek out information and review options. Deciding is an intensely personal process. But rare is the president who openly and consciously chooses to short-cut information. It is a fool's errand to act on instinct when information and data are available.

MY VIEW

Success is the result of effective leaders making good decisions and implementing them well. Both the individual *and* the institution matter.

To govern effectively, a president must put together *a team*. Not all teams play well together. In baseball, a good manager can bring the best out of his players. A bad manager can tear the team apart. Likewise, those who compose the team membership must be good at what they do, work well together, and follow the direction of the manager.

Skilled, experienced, strategic presidents are able to employ both the formal and informal elements of the president's arsenal. They recognize the pathogens likely to infect their efforts and are conscious of avoiding the minefields in their path. They utilize both the *personal* and the *institutional* sources of influence and power. They *persuade* and they *act* unilaterally. And they know when to persuade and bargain and when to exert direct presidential actions.

Legislation, especially landmark legislation, remains the presidential gold standard. A president's first choice should be, whenever possible, to attempt to develop a consensus, bargain with Congress, make necessary compromises, work to gain cooperation, and make deals. If that fails—and it often does— the president still has unilateral options.

But legislative success makes policy changes more permanent, stable, and difficult for a successor to undo. Where executive action can and often is reversed by a successor, laws tend to remain. And while several significant and long-lasting changes were instituted by unilateral presidential action (e.g., Kennedy created the Peace Corps, Truman desegrated the military), true staying power is most forcefully established via passage of laws.

CONCLUSION

Effective leaders know how to use institutions, not be used (or gobbled up) by them. Teams of clones (G. W. Bush), teams of rivals (Lincoln), teams of familiar veterans (Biden), or teams of strangers (Trump) all have an impact on presidential performance. Good leaders are also good managers.

The modern presidency is both the person and the institution.

3

DID THE FRAMERS INVENT A POWERFUL UNITARY EXECUTIVE OR A LIMITED CONSTITUTIONAL OFFICE?

I n a literal sense, the American presidency is a "unitary" office. That is, the Constitution establishes a single, unitary executive; one person *is* president. Article II of the Constitution is devoted to the newly invented presidency, and it opens with the words: "The executive Power shall be vested in a President of the United States of America."

This single sentence, known as the Vesting Clause, has started more arguments among presidency scholars than almost any other section in the Constitution. What did the framers mean— what was the "original intent" of this important sentence?

THE PROBLEM CLEARLY STATED

Is Article II, Section I, merely the conferring of a title ("President") to a single-person executive? Or, is it a grant of "all" executive power to that person? And if so, how is one to account for the several "executive" functions Article I grants to Congress? Words matter, and here, the framers might have been clearer. Were they really giving to the president "all" the executive power, some, or "most"?

On the basis of this single sentence, two very different under-standings of the scope of the president's powers have arisen. The *unitary theory* of executive power posits an expansive view of a president's powers that—it has been asserted—makes the president's acts, in the words of the George W. Bush administration, "non-reviewable" by Congress or the courts. But surely this cannot be. Ours is a separation-of-powers, checks-and-balances system where power is shared and overlapping. We did not fight a revolution against a hereditary king only to establish an elected king in America who possessed *all* executive power.

WHY IT MATTERS

The answer to this dilemma goes to the very heart of our con-stitutional republic. Is this a government of laws or men? Did we limit the executive or unleash it? Is the president above the law? Is the president *the law*? If the unitary theory is correct, the checks-and-balances, rule-of-law, limited-government model that we've been governed by for more than two hundred thirty years gives way to a model of executive dominance and indepen-dent power that defies, even undermines, the traditional separa-tion-of-powers, limited-government model.

Contrary to the separation-of-powers view, most unitary advocates would—in effect—make Richard Nixon's "when the president does it, that means it is not illegal," George W. Bush's claim that his actions in the war against terrorism are "non-reviewable," and Donald Trump's "I have the right to do whatever I want as president" binding and true. Surely this is not what the framers had in mind.

It should be noted that (1) not all unitary theory advocates go to these extremes (but many do), and (2) many unitary theory advocates promote their version of a "big" presidency not because that is what the Constitution provides for, but because it is that expansive model of executive powers they want to be in existence. They believe that we *need* a strong or dominant executive and thus claim (incorrectly, I believe) that one was created by the Constitution.[1]

THE RISE OF THE UNITARY THEORY

For more than two hundred years, the "unitary" aspect of the presidency posed no significant problem or controversy. Of course, the president was but one person at the head of one branch of government.

But something happened in the 1980s. With the presidency in the hands of conservative Ronald Reagan, some political conservatives who, since the 1930s and the rise of FDR and the New Deal, had opposed the development of the welfare state and a powerful presidency began to change their tunes. Having vigilantly opposed the rise of a big government and a big presidency, many conservatives began to imagine what a committed conservative might be able to do with a powerful presidency.[2]

Conservatives had already embraced a big government and a big presidency in the field of foreign affairs during the Cold War (roughly 1947 to 1989). In this era, conservatives supported a strong response to perceived challenges from the Soviet Union and in doing so sided with a powerful federal government in national security and a powerful presidency that could authoritatively lead the battle against Communism.

With the election of Ronald Reagan in 1980, many conservatives abandoned their small-government, small-presidency view, instead advocating for a big government and a big presidency—but how does one circle the philosophical square? Having railed against a powerful presidency for half a century, how might one justify this about-face?

Enter the unitary theory of the presidency. But we are getting ahead of ourselves. What did the inventors of the presidency create when they gave us a president of the United States?

START WITH THE FRAMERS

Let us start where one usually starts, at the beginning. After a revolution against the mightiest military nation on the face of the globe, after fighting that revolution primarily against executive tyranny in the form of a monarch, does it make sense that the framers would turn around and create a powerful, centralized executive in America?

In point of fact, the first Constitution—the Articles of Confederation and Perpetual Union—did not even have an executive officer. Congress could occasionally appoint a committee or person to fill an executive function, but there was no executive in the country's first Constitution.

This proved—not surprisingly—unworkable. The executive function required an executive entity, either one person or a set executive committee, usually referred to as a "plural executive."

Having experienced the inefficiency of the executive-less articles, the framers—some quite reluctantly—conceded that yes, an executive was necessary. But not just any executive. The framers attempted to establish an executive office that was compatible with *republican* government and values. And as no "republican executive" existed in the world, they had to invent one.[3]

And as we attempt to discern the intent of the framers in inventing this new *republican executive*, we should never lose sight of the fact that this Constitution was designed by men who were distrustful of both executive and governmental power.

The Constitution that emerged from the Constitutional Convention of 1787 in Philadelphia begins with Article I, devoted to the Congress. This article contains *most* of government powers and grants them not to the president but to Congress. To the framers, Congress was to be the more powerful branch of government.

Article II deals with the presidency. It creates a unitary office (one person) that would serve as the chief executive officer. The new executive's powers were not clearly spelled out, but most of those powers described in the Constitution required the president to share authority with others (especially the Senate). Reading the words of Articles I and II compel us to come away with a portrait of power wherein Congress holds most of the cards, but to act, *some cooperation* between the legislative and executive branches was necessary. Some type of consensus or agreement had to be reached; some accommodation between these two branches was required.

The framers created what amounts to an anti-leadership system of government. On the surface, this may sound unusual, but on reflection, it is clear that their goal, rather than to provide for an efficient system, was to create a government that would not jeopardize liberty. Thus, the men who invented the presidency created an executive institution that had *limited powers*.

The framers wanted to counteract two fears: the fear of the *mob* (democracy or mobocracy) and the fear of the *monarchy* (centralized, tyrannical executive power). The menacing image of England's King George III—against whom the colonists rebelled and whom Thomas Paine called the "Royal Brute of Britain"—served as a powerful reminder of the dangers of a strong executive.

To contain power, they set up an executive office that was constitutionally rather *weak*, dependent on the *rule of law*, and a *separation of powers* in order to ensure a system of *checks and balances*.

For James Madison, the chief architect of the Constitution, a government with too much power was a dangerous government. He believed that *human nature* drove men to pursue self-interest, and therefore a system of government designed to have "ambition check ambition" and power check power set within strict limits was the only hope to establish a stable government that did not endanger liberty. Realizing that "enlightened statesmen" would not always guide the nation, Madison embraced a check-and-balance system of separate but overlapping and shared powers. Madison's concern to have a government with controlled and limited powers is seen in Federalist no. 51, where he wrote, "You must first enable the government to control the governed; and in the next place, oblige it to control itself."

Of course, the government had to have enough power to govern, but it should not have enough power to overwhelm liberty. If one branch could check another, so the theory went, tyranny might be thwarted. But not all of the framers were this fearful of executive power. Alexander Hamilton emerged as the defender of a strong executive. Hamilton promoted, especially in the Federalist Papers, a version of executive power somewhat different from Madison's dispersed and separated powers. Madison wanted to check authority, Hamilton wished to support it; where Madison believed that the new government's powers should be "few and defined," Hamilton wanted to infuse the executive with "energy." Hamilton advocated vigorous government and a strong presidency. As Hamilton wrote in Federalist no. 70, good government requires "energy," and he simply rejected the weak executive: "A feeble executive implies a feeble execution of the government. A feeble execution is but another phrase for a bad execution; and a government ill-executed, whatever it may be in theory, must be, in practice, a bad government."

It is hard to argue with Hamilton's diagnosis, but what does he prescribe? What structure of power and government did the founders of the U.S. system design? The chief mechanisms they established to *control* as well as to *empower* the executive as mentioned in the introduction are as follows: (1) *limited constitutional government*, a reaction against the arbitrary, expansive powers of the king or state and a protection of personal liberty; (2) *rule of law*, so that only on the basis of legal or constitutional grounds could the government act; (3) *separation of powers*, so that the three branches of government each would have a defined sphere of power; and (4) *checks and balances*, so that each branch could limit or control the powers of the other branches of government. This new government required deal making, bargaining, and compromise. As Bill Clinton once said, the subtext of our Constitution is "let's make a deal."[4] In this sense, presidents must be negotiators, horse traders, and consensus builders.

Even Hamilton, the chief advocate for "energy" in the executive, envisioned that executive authority must exist *within* a republican form of government that separated and shared powers. The executive was not disembodied from the rest of the three-part government but was a part of that system. A republican executive had energy, but it was a particular form of energy, not apart from, but a part of and enmeshed in, the three-pronged government. Each branch would have its own spheres, but in order to check the other branches, some overlapping and sharing of authority was necessary. The president was not the errand boy of Congress, but neither was he its master.

THE UNITARY THEORY

As conservatives migrated from the limited presidency to the big presidency school of thought, they needed an intellectual justification for so dramatic a shift. They found (created) one in the new (they say, old) unitary theory of the executive.[5]

The goal: To establish a presidency-dominated system that—in an age of hyperchange and globalization—could powerfully and efficiently meet the needs of a twenty-first-century superpower. A stronger presidency was more likely to be able to deal with the demands of modernization by centralizing authority with unified control and diminishing the rivals to power (Congress and the courts), thereby allowing the president to lead with strength.

The means: To justify this presidential power-grab, a new theory had to be developed that traced its roots to the Founding era and argued that the *true* intent of the framers was to give to the president powers heretofore unrecognized in the American system. This new theory justified the creation of a more powerful presidency to govern in an age of globalization.

The argument: The central argument of the unitary school is that the framers created a powerful, independent presidency, one that was only marginally bound by the Madisonian checks and balances, in which *all* executive power belonged to the president. In one exhaustive examination of the unitary view, the authors conclude this is a theory that "ultimately values unilateral executive power over constitutional constraints." That theory posits the president of the United States controls the entire executive branch of the government and that he occupies a position of primacy in our constitutional system of separated powers and thus may exercise vast unilateral powers for the public good.

Presidents understandably want to have as much freedom to act as possible. However, presidents are often frustrated that our Constitution's system of separated powers and checks and balances delays or even derails their plans. Pro-executive political theorists have, over time, developed the unitary executive theory as a way not only to explain how presidents work around these constitutional constraints but also to justify such actions. In that way, the unitary executive theory is a normative view of the presidency used not only to describe presidential behavior but also to justify it.[6]

They further caution that:

The fundamental tenets of the unitary executive theory are not supported by core, constitutional principles of separation of powers and checks and balances. Nor is it a theory for which supporters can marshal empirical evidence that the American government currently, or ever, has adopted it as a working model that advances republican principles.[7]

And that:

Throughout US history, numerous presidents of course have taken aggressive or unilateral actions. Mostly these and other presidents who acted unilaterally did so under emergency circumstances (i.e., Civil War, Great Depression, and world wars) and never claimed that their extraordinary exercises of powers were permanent features of our governing system to be used anytime the president decides to do so. The unitary executive theory is different than the claim of temporary emergency powers belonging to presidents. The theory strikes at the very core of the ongoing operations of our delicately balanced system of powers among the branches of the national government.[8]

Pressure to develop this new theory began in the 1980s, when conservatives began to abandon their long-held suspicions of big government and a big, powerful presidency and began to believe that a strong presidency in the hands of a conservative president gave them the power needed to remake America's agenda and politics.[9]

While a modern theory, some advocates assert that it can actually be traced back to Alexander Hamilton, and that "all of our nation's presidents have believed in the theory of the unitary executive."[10] Yes, and no, depending on your definition of "unitary theory."

Yes, the presidency is a unitary office (headed by one person), but what is it beyond that? Unitary theory advocates (and they are not a monolithic group) cover a range of territory. Some— myself included—see the office as headed by a unitary figure who accrues some power by virtue of being the chief executive; others see the unitary nature of the office as granting the president full and complete executive power, or exclusive control over the executive branch; still others (see post–September 11 commentary) see a unitary executive as exercising substantial powers that are "non-reviewable" by the other branches.

The academic pedigree of the unitary executive claims to trace its roots back to the founding era, but this view was never the accepted position of the framers, nor was it written into the Constitution. In fact, a careful reading of Alexander Hamilton's writings in the Federalist Papers undermines many of the central claims of the unitary camp. The academic birth of the unitary executive grew out of several law journal articles promoting a new, originalist construction of the robust version of presidential power. These articles have given some academic legitimacy to the unitary executive theory, yet many conservatives are skeptical of this newly discovered originalist construction of expansive presidential power.

The unitary view sees presidential authority largely disembodied from the separation of powers and checks and balances and thus seems in contradiction to the original model of constitutionalism envisioned by the framers.

The unitary executive consists of six elements:

1. *Executive prerogative*, based on John Locke's *Second Treatise*.
2. *Energy in the executive*, grounded in Alexander Hamilton's defense of presidential authority.
3. The *coordinate construction* view of the Constitution, where the "executive power" or Vesting Clause is fused with the Commander-in-Chief Clause.
4. The *doctrine of necessity*, as practiced, for example, by Abraham Lincoln during the Civil War.
5. *Precedent*, or past practices of U.S. presidents.
6. Select *supporting court decisions*.

Modern-day unitary theorists see a Hobbesian world in which war and violence are the norm. Governments are thus created to provide order in a disorderly world. Who better to provide order, direction, and centralized leadership than the executive? The problem with the unitary advocates is that they believe the United States *must* have strong presidential leadership and so they *presume* this is what the framers would have given us—had they the knowledge and insight of today. But the framers had other goals in mind when creating the presidency. They wanted to prevent tyranny, not create a strong independent center of executive power.

Locke's executive prerogative. Political theorist John Locke had a significant impact on the framers. One view he espoused is that there are times when an executive may exercise extraordinary powers to meet grave dangers. The framers were well aware of this element of Locke's philosophy, and they were also aware that in republican Rome, the Senate could exercise a constitutional provision that temporarily transferred supreme power to a dictator who was empowered to solve the crisis. While the framers were aware of these two provisions, they chose not to include them in the Constitution. Strike one.[11]

Energy in the executive. Unitary advocates maintain that Alexander Hamilton promoted this view, and in some ways they may have a point. After all, Hamilton did promote an energetic executive. But again, Hamilton's energetic executive—as his writings in the Federalist Papers makes clear, was *republican* in nature and not independent of the other branches. As he wrote, in no. 70:

> There is an idea, which is not without its advocates, that a vigorous executive is inconsistent with the genius of republican government . . .
>
> Energy in the executive is a leading character in the definition of good government. It is essential to the protection of the community against foreign attacks: It is not less essential to the steady administration of the laws, to the protection of property against those irregular and high-handed combinations, which sometimes interrupt the ordinary course of justice, to the security of liberty against the enterprises and assaults of ambition, of faction and of anarchy . . . a feeble executive implies a feeble execution of the government. A feeble execution is but another phrase for bad execution. And a government ill executed, whatever it may be in theory, must be in practice a bad government . . .
>
> Taking it for granted, therefore, that all men of sense will agree in the necessity of an energetic executive, it will only remain to inquire, what are the ingredients which constitute this energy . . .
>
> The ingredients, which constitute energy in the executive, are first unity, secondly duration, thirdly an adequate provision for its support, fourthly competent powers.

Yes, Hamilton's view on the executive (Federalist nos. 67–77) suggests an energetic executive but one within a republican framework. Hamilton's is not an executive above the other branches but a part of a system of interlocking and shared powers. Strike two.

Coordinate construction. If one combines two Article II provisions of the Constitution, the Executive Power Clause (vesting power) and the Commander-in-Chief Clause, advocates of the unitary theory see a geometric expansion of executive authority where the parts, added together, multiply in significance, creating a prerogative authority for the president. Absent is the fact that the president also takes an oath of office to "preserve, protect, and defend the Constitution of the United States." And he must "take Care that the Laws be faithfully executed." This binds the president to the rule of law—laws passed by Congress.

Some unitary advocates argue that in times of crisis and war, an executive of virtually unchecked power is brought into existence. A September 25, 2002, Office of Legal Counsel (OLC) memo (written in the aftermath of the September 11 attack against the United States) argues that "these decisions [in wartime] under our Constitution are for the President alone to make." Other OLC memos suggest that in a crisis or war, the president may do things that are otherwise unlawful and that neither the Congress nor the courts have any authority to review presidential acts.

This expansive reading of the Constitution violates both the spirit and the letter of the law, and the Supreme Court, in cases such as *Hamdi v. Rumsfeld* (2004) and *Rasul v. Bush* (2004), and the Congress, in efforts such as its ban on the use of torture, have attempted to reclaim some of the power that was lost, delegated, ceded, or stolen. Perhaps a strike here as well.

The doctrine of necessity. While not a strictly legal doctrine, the claim of "necessity" has a practical application that can be quite persuasive. The old Roman adage *inter arma silent leges* ("in war, the laws are silent"), while not constitutionally valid, holds politically compelling force.

Certainly, the Constitution was *not* a suicide pact, and the doctrine of necessity asserts that a president might at times act beyond the scope of the Constitution. Lincoln was a servant of the law and the Constitution, even as he acted beyond their literal scope. He never claimed an inherent power to act beyond the law. Lincoln believed the authority of the government was, during a crisis, the authority to act in defense of the nation, knowing he was literally venturing on congressional territory. He never claimed that all authority was his, but that in a crisis, the doctrine of necessity might transfer authority to the government; authority that the president might exercise. "Must," he asked, "a government, of necessity, be too strong for the liberties of its own people or too weak to maintain its own existence?" No strike here.

The weight of precedent. That which was done by past presidents, unitary supporters argue, may legitimize such behavior for presidents who follow. When a president can say "as Lincoln and FDR did before me . . . ," he stands on the shoulders of giants and joins them in acts of boldness.

Lincoln during the Civil War, Woodrow Wilson in World War I, Franklin D. Roosevelt in both the Great Depression and World War II, George W. Bush in the war against terrorism, and others paved the path that a president may follow.

Precedent is, at best, of limited utility as a guide for extraconstitutional action. Repetition does not legalize that which is illegal. Strike, again.

Supportive court decisions. Overall, the courts have not served as a very effective check on presidential power. There have been times when the courts were willing to stand up to the president (e.g., some of the Civil War cases; early in the New Deal era; some Watergate cases; at times in the war against terrorism; and several times during the Trump presidency), but overall, the courts have tended to shy away from direct confrontations with presidents and were often willing to defer to a president or add to the powers of the office.

One case in particular speaks to the goals of the unitary theorist: *United States v. Curtiss-Wright Export Corp* (1936). In that case, Justice George Sutherland drew from a speech given in 1800 in the House of Representatives by then member of Congress and later to be chief justice John Marshall, who referred to the president as "the sole organ" of American foreign policy. This reference found its way into Sutherland's opinion and became a rallying cry for unitary advocates. Sutherland's "sole organ" remark was merely a judicial aside (dicta), yet it has become the unofficial executive branch mantra for the assertion of presidential power. Scholars have found little in *Curtiss-Wright* to rely on in the defense of the prerogative presidency, and apart from defenders of presidential power, this case is not seen as significant in granting presidents expansive powers. No strike here, but close.

A STORY

Historically, presidents have had to struggle to get Congress to pass their legislative proposals. For two hundred years, presidents and Congress battled for dominance, and for all but a few times prior to the Great Depression, Congress dominated. After all, the Constitution seems to grant superior powers to Congress, and comparatively speaking, the president's constitutional cupboard was rather bare. At least that was the accepted wisdom until fairly recently.

Beginning with the presidency of Ronald Reagan (1981–1989), conservatives, reflecting a growing recognition that traditionally small-government Republicans could better achieve their political goals via big government and a powerful presidency, began to assert that rather than the Constitution creating a limited executive, what it really created was a powerful unitary executive.[12]

While the idea of a unitary executive may have originated in the Reagan presidency, it first came into full practice in the presidency of George W. Bush (2001–2009). The predicate was the September 11 attack against the United States.

When the planes hit the Twin Towers in New York City, Americans turned to their president. "Do something!" they demanded. The White House sprang into action and Congress's power shrank, the courts waited on the sidelines, and the public called for executive action. Bush launched a war against the Taliban government of Afghanistan that had been harboring terrorist training camps.[13] He then declared a war against terrorism.

Extreme times may lead to or even justify extreme measures (see the doctrine of necessity). The terrorist attacks of September 11, 2001 became the driving argument allowing an intellectually threadbare theory of presidential unilateralism to assume center stage and attain a patina of legitimacy. But it must be remembered, the framers rejected Locke's broad prerogative in favor of a more restrictive system of checks and balances. They likewise rejected Hamilton's expansive executive for Madisonian checks and balances. While "necessity" is a powerful circumstantial argument, it is not a constitutional argument. Yes, the framers did, in Article II, give the president executive power, but it was not absolute.

Aided by a series of memos from the Office of Legal Counsel in the Bush Justice Department, the Bush administration governed during a crisis and wars in a manner imperial in style and unilateral in approach. And while the Congress did pass a joint resolution[14] authorizing Bush to engage U.S. forces against those responsible for the September 11 attack against the United States, Bush soon—and on his own claimed authority—expanded the war against terrorism beyond the September 11 perpetrators and waged a war in Iraq against Saddam Hussein that, while initially a quick military victory, soon got bogged down in an Iraqi internal war that proved long and tragic for Iraq and the United States.

And to prosecute that war and the war in Afghanistan, Bush resorted to the use of torture ("enhanced interrogation" in their jargon), set up secret detention centers, declared that the Geneva Accords did not apply to the United States, allowed for the mistreatment and denial of legal rights of detainees and U.S. citizens, and other acts.[15]

In order to justify broad assertions of power, the Bush administration offered a bold new theory of presidential power: the unitary theory. But this theory overstates its case and ignores the words of the framers. That the Bush administration was able to act as a unitary theory executive, with boldness as well as unilateral actions, speaks to the political, not the constitutional, realities.

George W. Bush acted like a president whose actions were justified by a theory that armed him with unrestrained powers. He became the embodiment of a unitary executive as defined by modern conservatives. Perhaps surprisingly, Congress too acted as if the unitary theory were valid. The courts, however, on some significant issues, decided against several of Bush's policies on detainee rights and other anti-terrorism-related matters. The public, unaware of the consequential debate regarding the scope of presidential power, demanded presidential action.

The institutional incapacity of Congress certainly factors in on its relative inability to confront a president, but an absence of will also plays into this. Congress is not completely docile, but it seems to have given up the fight and ceded to the president constitutional territory belonging to Congress.

Thus, President Bush's claims to power, as well as his bold exercise of executive power, were circumstantial and political, and not constitutional or legal. And for us to willingly embrace this constitutional fiction does violence to the Constitution and is pregnant with menace. That Bush got away with exercising such bold action is not a testimony to the president's sound constitutional arguments—they were largely bogus—but to the political demands and opportunities presented by the September 11 attack. About that animating situation, Congress might have been more assertive in pressing its institutional as well as constitutional authority.

MY VIEW

I find the unitary executive theory—at least the extreme version promoted by many conservatives—to be a groundless view, not supported by the evidence or logic. It serves as a description of presidential behavior, while it is also used to justify actions beyond republican standards.[16]

Why would the framers fight a war against executive authority, only to create a mighty presidential office that could easily become monarchical? The framers created a limited office under the *rule of law* in a system of *shared* and *overlapping* powers. Unitary? Yes, but primarily in the sense that they created a single or unitary office to head the executive branch of government. Yes, Article II, Section I, makes the executive a "president," and it assigns to this new executive office administrative or executive authority, but it also, in Article I, assigns certain "executive functions" to Congress as well. In fact, the very theory of American government is grounded in a shared model of power.

Today's unitary theory advocates may not like the fragmentation of power inherent in our system, and it certainly *is* a slow, deliberative process that usually ends in deadlock, and yes, problems mount and solutions are rare, but those conditions do not justify the abandonment of constitutional principles because we *wish* the framers had given us a more presidency-centered Constitution. The Constitution shares and overlaps powers; wishing it were not so does not make it go away. You want a stronger presidency? Change the Constitution. But the fiction that the framers created a big, powerful presidency does constitutional violence and carries with it irredeemable consequences. The constitutional presidency—like it or not—is a limited presidency.

CONCLUSION

The emergence of the unitary theory of the executive parallels the rise of populism across the globe. As globalization and hyperchange created instability, disruptive politics, and the rise of populism, those protest and oppositional forces confronted the perceived fault lines or limitations of liberal democracy, offering a form of illiberal democracy as a replacement.

The stakes are high, the results consequential. Do we defend the liberal democracy the framers established or do we revise and/or reform that system to strengthen the executive at the expense of our checks-and-balances system to allow for a more efficient and more centralized form of leadership under the control of a single person?

If we do so, what would we gain and what would we lose? And is the status quo really so bad that major surgery is the only remedy? Would reform, deform? And what might be the "unintended consequences" of such a change? The unitary theory seeks to make this dramatic change without going through the actual legal or constitutional process of change. Its advocates would *like* the presidency to be stronger (as would I, as a matter of fact), but instead of admitting (as some do) that the invention of a powerful executive *was not* the design of the framers, they still insist it *should be* brought into existence, in the twenty-first century, for the world's only superpower. Many would skip the hard work of persuading us to make this change and merely assert "it was always so." It was not.[17]

Let us have the debate, then decide.

4

WHICH IS MORE VALUABLE, CHARACTER OR COMPETENCE?

What *should* we want of our presidents? Superman or everyman? One of the many paradoxes of the presidency is that we simultaneously want contrasting, even contradictory qualities in our presidents. We want a leader who is bold and leads with conviction yet also enacts our will; we yearn for a decisive leader yet one who won't be too strong and threaten the checks and balances of our system; we want a decent, honorable president who at times will be cunning and at times even ruthless; we want a president who will solve our problems but not ask sacrifices of us.[1] As Supreme Court justice David Souter noted, "The Constitution embodies the desire of the American people, like most people, to have things both ways. We want order and security, and we want liberty."[2]

We demand that our presidents be of the highest moral character and conduct themselves as paragons of our highest values, demonstrating behavior that serves as an example and model for our children to follow. Our president must be morally "good."

But of course, it is a rough, dangerous world out there, and at times our adversaries may wish us harm. At such times, we want a president who will stand up for our interests and promote our safety. This may sometimes mean that a president will order troops into battle where Americans will kill and be killed. And at home, the hyper-partisanship of politics sometimes means that a president will need to play hardball, manipulate others, dissemble where necessary, and at times practice the "dark arts." So, what do we want, character or competence? (Spoiler alert: we want both.)

Must the president be a "good" person to be a "good" president? Are we electing a pastor or a president whose job it is to save our souls or save our nation? Do we want a master of soulcraft or of statecraft?

Yes, in an ideal world we would have both, but the real world provides no such opportunity. If the choices were easy, they would have been solved before they reached the president's desk. Only the most vexing of problems become presidential decisions. At times, presidents must make tough choices about following high moral principles or protecting American interests.

THE PROBLEM CLEARLY STATED

What do we really *want* and *need* in our presidents, goodness or effectiveness? Someone who will morally elevate us or skillfully exercise power on our behalf? Someone we respect and admire or someone who can get the job done?

WHY THIS QUESTION IS IMPORTANT

If we honor, praise, and reward moral goodness in our presidents, that is what they will strive to provide us with. If we admire a president who gets the job done (no matter what), who is willing to cut corners to win, that is what we will get. Our answers to these questions will determine, to a large extent, the type of president we get.

Franklin D. Roosevelt said that the presidency "is preeminently a place of moral leadership." And we tend to think it so. We want our presidents to be honorable and moral. We want them to appeal to our better angels, to lead democratically and justly. But when the republic is threatened, as it was after September 11, we want our president to be an avenging angel who will protect our homeland and smite our enemies.

Saint and sinner. Today we want one, tomorrow the other.

OF SAINTS AND SINNERS IN THE WHITE HOUSE, OR ALL OUR HEROES HAVE FEET OF CLAY

Is there a connection between a person's public and private character? Can a president be of the highest character in private life and yet be a corrupt and venal president? Conversely, can a person whose private life is littered with morally questionable acts be a moral president? Another way of approaching the dilemma is to ask: Is character a predictor of performance? Must a flawed person be a flawed president, and are our moral presidents our most effective presidents?

Many of the traits or behaviors that seem to lead to success seem counter to the practice of highly moral people. Stubbornness, disagreeableness, and being pushy, ambitious, assertive, and willing to dissemble and use the tools of manipulation often lead to victory. Kindness, idealism, modesty, and altruism may be fine qualities in my friends and neighbors but might not always be helpful for a president determined to get his way.

We need not focus on the extreme cases (e.g., Gerald Ford and Jimmy Carter as highly moral but politically limited presidents or, conversely, Donald Trump, who was both venal and ineffective). What ethical problems do *most* of our presidents face, and how do they deal with these problems? And in calculating a response to problems, do they weigh questions of character versus competence?

We all wear masks; we all try to present to the world an imagine of ourselves we want others to see. Yet, we are not always as we seem. Plus, all our heroes have feet of clay. Somewhere along the way, we've all done things about which we are not proud. If we judge others by too exact a set of standards—perfection, for example—no one will pass that test. As the Zen koan reminds us, "water that is too pure, has no fish." So, what are reasonable parameters for presidential behavior? And as Abraham Lincoln noted, "It has been my experience that folks who have no vices generally have very few virtues."

More than most offices, the presidency is a highly personalized office. It bends to meet the occupant. And while there are certain norms and expectations, demands and roles all presidents are supposed to follow, individual variations are important. The "locus" of the presidency matters. The presidency is responsive to the different styles and personalities of the people who occupy the office. As former Lyndon Johnson aide George Reedy, who served one of the quirkiest of the modern presidents, noted: "In the White House, character and personality are important because no other limitations govern a man's conduct. Restraint must come from within the presidential soul and prudence from within the presidential mind. The adversary forces that temper the actions of others do not come into play until it is too late to change course." He added, "His character is the key to his success or failure in terms of history more than his ability to do the job."[3]

Is character everything? Or are results the key? Rectitude or outcomes? And if the best person is not the best president, does goodness trump performance? Do we want our presidents to be good or good at the job?[4]

Some of our most highly regarded presidents engaged in highly questionable behavior. Abraham Lincoln was no saint. As the Steven Spielberg movie *Lincoln* (2012) suggests, Honest Abe could be a wheeler-dealer who sometimes made shady deals, directed to fine purposes perhaps, but he used questionable means to achieve honorable goals.[5]

FDR was no angel. He could dissemble with the best of them; he was a master manipulator. But FDR and Lincoln employed their considerable talents—of both light and darkness—toward noble and selfless ends. They could cut deals, engage in a game of political jiu jitsu, mislead and misdirect, yet their eyes were always focused not on what best served *their* needs, but what served the nation's needs. They may have employed the dark arts now and then, but always toward an honorable ideal. Paradox? You bet (figure 4.1).

Machiavelli is widely interpreted as espousing all brands of corruption and manipulation. But he does not call for manipulation for manipulation's sake. To Machiavelli, the only leaders

		Character	
		High	Low
Competence	High	Barack Obama	Lyndon Johnson Richard Nixon
	Low	Jimmy Carter Gerald Ford	Donald Trump Warren Harding

FIGURE 4.1 The character/competence matrix

who deserve honor and praise are those who achieve honorable results by honorable means. Moses was one such figure. Those who deserve our scorn are leaders who achieve selfish ends via corrupt means. Most real-world leaders fall somewhere in between these two extremes.

The prince must pursue what is best for the state. That this in part means what is best for him (accumulate and use power, sometimes ruthlessly) is a consequence of positioning himself to secure his polity's safety and security. The ends justifying the means? No. The ends (if they are "good") may at times necessitate (and only when necessary) that the prince dirty his hands in the service of the best interests of the people. The prince should not do this just to gain power, but to gain power so that he may govern more effectively and more justly.

VIRTUE AND VIRTUES

One particularly useful way to understand the complexity of this issue is to ask just what do we mean by goodness in a political context. Fortunately, most of the heavy lifting on this question has already been done for us by Harvard University political scientist Dennis F. Thompson. In exploring questions of presidential character, Thompson draws a distinction between three different virtues. We can look at *private virtues*, *public virtues*, and *constitutional virtues*. "Which virtues," he asks, "should have priority"?

Thompson makes the persuasive case that constitutional virtues, or constitutional character, matters most. He defines this as "the disposition to act, and to motivate others to act, according to the principles that constitute the democratic process." These include a sensitivity to basic rights, respect for due process, willingness to accept responsibility, tolerance of opposition, and a commitment to candor. So, is our top priority finding a president who is committed to constitutional virtues? That would be my position.[6]

WHY WE FALL SHORT

Is it power? Or is it human nature? Why do we so often stray or fall short of our best selves? We all know Lord Acton's famous quote "power corrupts, and absolute power corrupts absolutely." And there is considerable merit to his cautionary insight. Power *does* something to a person. But what? Abraham Lincoln supplies us with an answer to that question: *power reveals*. As George Reedy reminds us: "In reality, the office neither elevates nor degrades a man. What it does is to provide a stage upon which all of his personality traits are magnified and accentuated. The aspects of his character that were not noted previously are not new. They were merely hidden from view in lesser positions, where he was only one of many politicians competing for public attention."[7]

Yes, power goes to our heads; but power also opens a door into our psyches. I have a rule: the person who most *wants* to be department chair should *never* be given the job. I learned this from experience. Beware of the power-hungry at universities and in life. They are usually motivated by inner demons and driven by darker impulses. The best chair is the (truly) reluctant chair, the one who does the job to serve, not to wield power.

We humans are a mixed up, complicated breed. And presidents seek power and position for a variety of reasons. The framers of the Constitution held a fairly jaundiced view of human nature, and this is nowhere more clearly revealed than in their separation-of-powers, checks-and-balances system. Presidents needed checks upon power. Hard experience taught this lesson. The framers' fear of tyranny, sometimes referred to a tyranno-phobia, led them to set up a system that set ambition off against ambition, and power off against power.

A STORY

Presidents Jimmy Carter[8] and Gerald Ford[9] were—it has been widely recognized—honorable and decent men. Yet, both were largely ineffective presidents. Bill Clinton, on the other hand, was a scalawag.[10] Yet, he was an astute politician and a reason-ably effective president. Richard Nixon, arguably one of the two most corrupt presidents in history, nonetheless could be a brilliant strategist and practitioner of realpolitik.[11] Would-be president Hillary Clinton was exceptionally well qualified and effective, yet questions of character plagued her and contrib-uted to her 2016 loss to Donald Trump.[12] And what can one say of the character of Donald Trump?[13] The *Washington Post* fact checkers found that in his four years as president, Trump told over thirty-five thousand lies.[14]

Is it character or competence? Which president is recognized as a truly honorable man and a truly exceptional president? Of the three presidents rated as "great," Washington, Lincoln, and FDR, only Washington comes at all close to our "good person–good president" level. Both Lincoln and FDR could be duplici-tous, be manipulative, cut shady deals, practice both the high and low arts of politics, dissemble, and lie when it served a purpose.

Just how "good" (morally) do we want our presidents to be? Or do we really want our presidents to be highly effective—as long as they aren't "too" immoral? During the impeachment trial of Bill Clinton, the case against his character was clear and unassailable: While president, he was unfaithful to his wife with a twenty-one-year-old White House intern, lied about it, lied under oath about it, attempted to cover up his indiscretion, and may have obstructed justice. And yet, during that time of *peace and prosperity*, the public was not only willing to forgive and forget but also supported Clinton with a job approval rating in the 60 percent range.

And when Donald Trump faced his first and second impeachments (the first during a period of relative peace and prosperity)—both cases against Trump were highly convincing: he *did* misuse his power to pressure a foreign leader to dig up dirt on his likely 2016 presidential rival Joe Biden and then he *did* incite an insurrection against the government of the United States that led to the storming of the Capitol and the deaths of several law enforcement officials—the Senate failed to convict.

Contrast Clinton and Trump with Carter and Ford. Gerald Ford became president when Richard Nixon, facing the certainty of impeachment and conviction over Watergate-related crimes, resigned. Ford—an exceedingly decent man—suffered from the Nixon fallout and, although he had a spotless character, suffered from guilt-by-association with Nixon. The public was in a presidency-bashing mood, and the president who bore the brunt of public disdain was Gerald Ford. His hands tied, Ford was unable to exercise the powers of the presidency, and he failed in his 1976 effort to win the office himself.

Jimmy Carter followed Ford into the White House. But the Watergate effect was still a profound force, and in spite of Herculean efforts, Carter faced a public still in a presidency-bashing mood and a Congress unwilling to follow the lead of a president. Carter's many positive efforts (e.g., energy) often fell flat as suspicions of any and all executives poisoned the political well and inhibited presidential leadership. In a time of economic trouble and an oil shortage, Carter asked us to make sacrifices for the public good. That message proved toxic in a consumer-dominated culture. Ford and Carter refused to pander to the public. They paid a high price.

What message do we send when we support scalawags who provide us with *bread and circuses*[15] yet reject honorable leaders who ask us to make necessary sacrifices?

Florentine diplomat and political philosopher Niccolò Machiavelli (1469–1527) would have understood this conundrum. He had a realistic (some would say jaundiced) view of politics. While politics was a way of solving collective problems of governing, it was also the art of the possible, and at times the art of guile and manipulation.

In *The Prince*, his classic treatise on how to gain and use power, Machiavelli instructs the prince to deal with others not as they should be but as they are. This means some adversaries will be deceitful and attempt to cause harm and take advantage of the prince. Thus, the prince must be prepared—when circumstances demand—to do "that which is not good"—to protect both his own power but also to protect the interests of the people and the polity.

Does this same rule apply to the president? And if so, do we want our presidents to be morally pure or politically effective?

MY VIEW

Playwright T. S. Eliot, in his play *The Cocktail Party*, has one of his characters say the line, "Half the harm that is done in the world is due to people who want to feel important."[16] Many would-be leaders are drawn to the world of politics because that is where the power is. It is an intoxicant. Lording over others can be a rush. In Eliot's words, it makes them "feel important."

But politics is about more than power. It is also about serving. It is about trying to achieve justice. It is about community building. But even the most high-minded of politicians know that they must at times use power to achieve their noble ends.

Character or power; honor or competence? Put starkly, it is an either/or choice that forces us to choose from the extremes. But real-world politics is lived between the black and white, in the gray areas of more-or-less, rather than right or wrong. Power is what you do. Character is who you are.

So, how do we judge presidents on the craft/competence scale? One thing seems clear: we should not too harshly judge a politician by a single *isolated act*. Better to look instead for patterns of behavior. How is character revealed? Sometimes the simplest things reveal the most. When asked the same question ("Have you smoked marijuana?"), three different modern presidents answered in the following ways:

Bill Clinton: "I didn't inhale."
George W. Bush: "I will not elaborate on the mistakes of my youth."
Barack Obama (asked if he inhaled): "Well, that's kind of the point, isn't it?"

Following are some of the questions we *should* ask regarding presidents:

Is "private" character a predictor of behavior in the White House?
• No.
Must one be a good person to be a good leader?
• No, we find no such correlation.
How did they deal with loss or adversity?
• When most vulnerable and disappointed, were they a good sport or a bad sport, a good loser or a bad loser?

Did they appeal to the better angels within us?

- To what means of appeal and motivation did they resort?

Did they try to bring out the best or the worst in us?

- Were we sheep to manipulate or citizens to enlighten?

How much of a sacrifice to character must we make in order to get a high degree of competence? We have a right to expect both, but we must also be sensitive to the nuances of the case, to complexity, to competing values, and to the hierarchies of values. Life—especially political life—is lived in the gray areas.[17]

In the end, Aristotle seems to have given us the best answer. The leader should strive to achieve *phronesis*. This refers to *knowledge* put to *appropriate action* toward achieving a *worthy goal*. It is about knowing what to do, knowing why it needs to be done, how it can be done, what opportunities and roadblocks we face, what the political environment's limits might be, how to get the most out of limited opportunities, and how to direct actions toward a moral and worthy goal.

CONCLUSION

Baltasar Gracián, seventeenth-century Jesuit philosopher and theologian, wrote of "the art of undertaking things. Fools rush in through the door—for folly is always bold. . . . But prudence enters with more deliberation. Its forerunners are caution and care; they advance and discover whether you can also advance without danger."[18]

Get as much as you can of the worthy goal you seek, but know the limits, know the road down which you should not go, and be boldly cautious, ethically alert, and situationally aware. Inside the Obama administration they had a mantra: "Don't do stupid shit." I couldn't have said it better myself.

Former George W. Bush speechwriter Michael Gerson, writing in the *Washington Post*, noted the broad impact of presidential character:

> Politics does not directly determine the morality of citizens. But it helps shape the system of social cues and stigmas in which citizens operate. It matters where leaders delegitimize hatred or fertilize it, if they isolate prejudice or mainstream it. If political figures base their appeal on the cultivation of resentment for some group or groups, they are releasing deadly toxins into our society without any idea who might be harmed or killed. Such elected leaders might not have blood on their hands directly, but they are creating a society with more bloody hands.[19]

5

WHAT IS MORE IMPORTANT, SKILL OR OPPORTUNITY?

Most Americans believe that skill is the key ingredient in presidential success. If only President X had more political skill, had a better power sense, knew how to move the pieces on the presidential chessboard more effectively, he or she would be better able to set the agenda, garner popular support, pressure Congress to follow his or her lead, and get the bureaucracy to implement the president's programs. If only . . .

When leaders who have been highly successful at several jobs prior to their time in the White House do poorly, we are left to wonder: Where is the skill that brought them so much success in their previous jobs? An effective governor, an empire-building businessperson, a highly decorated military hero, we have had them all, and even their successful backgrounds did not necessarily translate into success in the presidency.

So, is skill enough? How important is skill in determining success? Lyndon Johnson was considered a master politician. He engineered landmark civil rights, voting rights, and education legislation. Was it because he was so skilled or because he had huge partisan majorities in both houses of Congress? Or was it because the public strongly supported said legislation? Did a social movement prepare the way for federal reforms? What then, is the role of agency in presidential success; what is the answer to the causation question?[1]

THE PROBLEM CLEARLY STATED

What is the more important prerequisite to presidential success, the skill of the president or circumstances (context or opportunity)? Do presidents set the table or do they try to work from a table already set? Is presidential leadership similar to a card game where you are dealt a hand and that is your starting point in the game of power? If you are dealt three aces, you need do little to improve your hand—the game is likely yours. But if you are dealt a weak hand (a three and seven of spades, a two and six of clubs, a jack of hearts, and a nine and queen of diamonds), you must work hard to improve your position and, even so, are not likely to win this game.

WHY THIS QUESTION MATTERS

Knowing the answer to this question allows a president to more efficiently assess or diagnose the situation and choose a style or approach best suited to that particular context. Presidents are thus more likely to adapt to the situation and less apt to apply the wrong cure to the problem.

THE VARIABLE NATURE OF PRESIDENTIAL POWER, OR THE GOLDILOCKS DILEMMA REVISITED

Earlier, we introduced the reader to the Goldilocks dilemma. Let us explore it more deeply. We are all familiar with the children's story of *Goldilocks and the Three Bears.* Goldilocks, tired and hungry having walked through the forest, chances upon a house, but no one is home. She looks into a window and sees three bowls of porridge. Overcome by hunger, she enters the house and tries the first bowl: "This porridge is too hot" she declares. She moves onto the second bowl, but "This porridge is too cold." Upon trying the third bowl, she exclaims with joy: "This porridge is *just right.*"

That is the way it is with presidential power: sometimes it is too hot (during a crisis or when dealing with foreign policy); sometimes it is too cold (when focusing on domestic or economic policy); only rarely do we get it "just right" (as when a president has a large partisan majority in Congress and develops a wide-ranging consensus).

This story suggests that—if true—conditions, context, or circumstances are more important in determining a president's power than the political skill of that president. This chapter will try to settle that question.

USEFUL DISTINCTIONS: SKILL AND OPPORTUNITY

Clearly skill matters, but when, why, and how? As discussed in the introduction, Niccolò Machiavelli saw three factors determining success: *virtù* (skill), *occasione* (opportunity), and *fortuna* (luck). We have no control over fortune, but skill is under our control. Opportunity is not.

Presidential power is not fixed or stable; it is variable and dynamic (see the related text box), and it matters greatly whether the president governs in *normal* times, when there is relative serenity and calm, or in a crisis or emergency. In normal times, the full force of the separation-of-powers and checks-and-balances system inhibits presidential power. But in a crisis or emergency, the normal checks on a president fade, and presidents are granted significant authority (see the related text box). Thus, power presupposes a *predicate* that opens or closes the door to power. Presidential success means applying skill to the circumstances at hand. In a crisis, presidents can do much; in normal times, they are greatly constrained.

PRESIDENTIAL POWER

High flex/high flux
Variable and elastic
Conditional (crisis vs. routine)
Personal (skill level)
Constrained (constitution/rule of law)
Systemic (separation of powers)
Dynamic not static

NORMAL CONDITIONS VERSUS EMERGENCY CONDITIONS

Normal conditions	Emergency conditions
Separation of powers	Separation of powers diminished
Presidency	Presidency on steroids
Sisyphus	Leviathan
Balance of powers	Imperial presidency
Checks and balances	Monarchial prerogative
Rule of law	Unilateralism

SKILL

Skill matters. In sports, car repair, brain surgery, teaching, and the presidency, skill matters. Of course. But when, and how, and to what degree?

Many presidential scholars argue that "if we could only get the *right person* in the White House, most of our problems would evaporate." Historian Arthur Schlesinger Jr. challenges these structuralists, who argue that the separation of powers inhibits strong leadership. Instead, he believes that highly skilled presidents have been able to overcome the structural roadblocks. He writes:

> Is the difficulty we encounter these days in meeting our problems really the consequences of defects in the structure of our government? After all, we have had the separation of powers from the beginning of the republic. This has not prevented competent presidents from acting with decision and dispatch. The separation of powers did not notably disable Jefferson or Jackson or Lincoln or Wilson or the Roosevelts. . . . The real difference is that the presidents who operated the system successfully knew what they thought should be done—and were able to persuade Congress and the nation to give their remedies a try. . . . Our problem is not at all that we know what to do and are impeded from doing it by some structural logjam in the system. Our problem—let us face it—is that we don't know what to do.[2]

No scholar is more identified with the skill argument than Richard Neustadt. His 1960 book, *Presidential Power*, is still considered one of the most important books ever written about presidential politics. Neustadt recognizes that the system or structure of American government is designed to frustrate presidential leadership and argues that to overcome these roadblocks, presidents must make optimal use of their informal resources: skill, prestige, reputation. Only then can presidents solve the "power problem" of the American system.

The most important skill a president needs is good *judgment*. By contrast, the most important skill the average person can have is *empathy*. Empathy ranks second, behind sound judgment, in the list of important presidential skills. Among the other skills a president needs are the following:

- Emotional intelligence
- Strong cognitive abilities
- Stamina
- Passion for problem-solving
- Curiosity
- Character
- Drive/ambition
- Courage of conviction
- Intellectual capacity
- Electoral experience
- Compassion
- Communication skills
- Theatrical self-promotion
- Perspective
- Crisis management skills

- Ability to recognize and empower talented subordinates
- Legislative experience
- Listening skills
- Decision-making skills
- Managerial experience
- Self-awareness
- Power sense
- Bargaining skills
- Persuasive skills
- Optimism
- Sound temperament
- Openness
- Flexibility/adaptability
- Humility
- Integrity
- Consensus and coalition building

In *The Presidential Dilemma*, I described it thus:

> To be successful, a president must be a jack-of-all-trades *and* a
> master of all! It *is* rocket science. Since power floats in the United
> States, since it is so elusive, a power vacuum is the natural order,
> and someone or something fills it. Usually, the vacuum is filled by
> those who wish to protect the status quo: As protectors of what is,
> they have most of the advantages over the advocates of change. In
> the United States, there is a great deal of *negative power*, multiple
> veto points, but few opportunities to promote change.
>
> Many rivals attempt to fill the power void, but no one is better
> situated to do so than the president. In effect, the presidency is
> the only "modern" institution of government. The Congress acts
> slowly; the Court must wait for a case to arrive. But the presidency
> is a modern institution in the sense that it can move quickly, react
> with speed and dispatch; it can decide. In this sense, the Con-
> gress adapts poorly, while the presidency can adapt quickly. As
> the world becomes smaller, as communication becomes almost
> instantaneous, as travel speeds up, as technology progresses, the
> perceived need to move quickly, adapt, and adjust heightens.
> The presidency, with a single hand at the helm, can move, can fill
> the power vacuum.[3]

The model of the skilled president remains Franklin D. Roosevelt. He was able to perform the alchemy that turned opportunity into power. Historian Arthur Schlesinger Jr. wrote of him:
"He was forever weighing questions of personal force, of political timing, of congressional concern, of partisan benefit, of public
interest. Situations had to be permitted to develop, to crystallize,
to clarify; the competing forces had to vindicate themselves in
the actual pull and tug of conflict; public opinion had to face the
question, consider it, pronounce upon it—only then, at the long,

frazzled end, would the President's intuitions consolidate and precipitate a result."[4]

FDR loved politics and believed in himself. He was the most political of political animals, always eyeing his goal as he assessed where he was, where he wanted to go, how best to get there, and how to leverage available resources to meet the demands of the situation. Cold. Calculating. Manipulative. And masterful.[5]

FDR was an experienced insider, and experience matters. He had been a New York state senator, assistant secretary of the navy during World War I, and James M. Cox's vice-presidential running mate in 1920. In 1921 FDR contracted polio, and his legs were fully paralyzed. Undeterred, he became governor of New York in 1929, and he was elected president in 1932.

In recent years, Americans, critical of the inside-the-Beltway performance of professional career politicians, often looked to outsiders for salvation. In the post-Vietnam, post-Watergate era, we devalued experience and wanted someone who was not "corrupted" by D.C. politics. How well have the outsiders done (table 5.1)?

TABLE 5.1 POST-VIETNAM, POST-WATERGATE PRESIDENTS

Year(s) elected	Name	Party	Experience [political/military]	Historical rank	In-Out
'76	Jimmy Carter	D	State legislator and governor, Georgia	Low	Outsider
'80, 1984	Ronald Reagan	R	Governor, California	Medium	Outsider
'88	George H. W. Bush	R	Vast experience	Medium	Insider
'92, 1996	Bill Clinton	D	Governor, Arkansas	Medium	Outsider
2000, 2004	George W. Bush	R	Governor, Texas	Low	Outsider
2008, 2012	Barack Obama	D	State legislator, Illinois senator	Medium/high	Outsider
2016	Donald Trump	R	None	Low	Outsider
2020	Joe Biden	D	Vast experience	—	Insider

Eight presidents, twelve presidential terms, two insiders, six outsiders. Is it a coincidence that the outsiders rank below the insiders in expert evaluations of their presidencies? or that limited experience has also led to lower ratings?

Donald Trump was the ultimate outsider. The only president in U.S. history with no political and no military experience, Trump prided himself on being an outsider and disruptor. But disrupting is one thing; building up, quite another. Trump tried to repeal or destroy Obamacare, but had no plan to replace it with anything. Populists, outsiders, and disruptors are more appealing when on the outside, shouting in. But once in office and responsible for the job of governing, they face handicaps that inhibit their ability to perform and often prove quite disappointing.

POLITICAL OPPORTUNITY

How and to what extent does opportunity shape the parameters of presidential success? Presidency scholars have identified two broad areas where context matters greatly: in the distinction between domestic and foreign policy and between crisis and normal situations.

In 1966, political scientist Aaron Wildavsky published an influential essay titled "The Two Presidencies." The essay opens with the line, "The United States has one president, but it has two presidencies, one presidency is for domestic affairs, and the other is concerned with defense and foreign policy."[6] Presidents have considerable power over foreign affairs but very limited power in the domestic arena. A powerful president abroad, a weak president at home.

Wildavsky's work has come under considerable scrutiny, yet it has held up over time. While presidents do not have a blank check in foreign affairs, they do exercise considerable power. Thus, in foreign policy, presidents usually can control both process and policy.

In the domestic arena, both the Congress and the public claim greater knowledge, higher interest, and more power to impact both process (interest-group politics) and policy (domestic matters more directly affect the public and are more closely linked to public support for members of Congress who "take care of them"). Context matters.

The other area where power is quite variable is the crisis/normal conditions dyad. In a crisis, the public demands that a president take over and solve the problem. Congress too looks to the president and cedes considerable power to whoever is president. Take September 11. When the United States was attacked and we watched first the South Tower then the North Tower crumble, taking nearly three thousand lives, virtually everyone looked to President Bush and demanded that he provide both justice and revenge. Bush obliged and felt free enough to order agents of the U.S. government to go well beyond the law (e.g., engage in torture). For nearly two years, Bush ruled (almost) alone. Like the king of old, his word *became* policy.

Crisis creates opportunities. "There are times," Abigail Adams wrote to her son John Quincy in 1780, "in which a Genius would wish to live. It is not in the still calm of life, or the repose of a pacific station, that great characters are formed. Would Cicero have shone so distinguished an orator, if he had not been roused, kindled and enflamed by the Tyranny of Catiline, Millo, Verres and Mark Anthony."[7]

The ambitious Theodore Roosevelt regretted that he did not enter the arena during a crisis, knowing that a "great occasion" allowed for a "great statesman" to emerge. Great occasions do not create great leaders, but they do create great opportunities for leaders to lead greatly.

Machiavelli recognized this when he wrote of the need for *occasione* to give the prince the opportunity to demonstrate his *virtù*. Without the opportunity, *virtù* (skill) remains largely dormant.

A PRESIDENT'S "LEVEL OF POLITICAL OPPORTUNITY"

Presidents generally enjoy the most success at passing legislation in year one. In fact, in "all" political systems, year one is almost always the time of the most significant change.[8] In year one, the opposition is taking the measure of the new president. The public—or at least a portion of them—is pulling for the new president to succeed, and new hope and new policies come into play.

But not all presidencies are created equal. Some new presidents come in with a clear mandate to govern. But most don't. A mandate is a warrant to take action. A presidential mandate is the informal granting of the authority to carry out the agenda upon which the president ran. But few presidents come into office with a clear mandate to govern. A mandate is calculated (informally) by measuring an incoming president's level of political opportunity.[9]

Among the key factors in calculating a new president's level of political opportunity are the following:

- Margin of electoral victory

- Type of election

- Number of president's party in Congress

- Presidential coattails

- Political/management experience

- Communication skills

- Public demand for action

- Trust in government
- Nature of political opposition
- Match of political time to presidents

- Issues in congressional pipeline
- Level of public trust in government

To what extent do opportunities or circumstances shape a president's leadership possibilities? Are presidents bound by circumstances or can they shape the agenda and political opportunities to favor their positions? Not all times are created equal. There are moments when the public demands governmental action; at other times the political pendulum swings from a public in an activist phase to a public skeptical of governmental activity and resistant to change. Likewise, events may press the government to act as was the case after September 11 and during the COVID-19 crisis.

Thus, we ask: Are circumstances and events the "super sauce" that emboldens and empowers leaders at some points and limits them at other points?

High-opportunity presidents have a much greater chance of gaining political victories than do low-opportunity presidents.[10] And when we link up skill and opportunity, we see the times when presidents are more likely to succeed. A presidency may have high or low skill and face high or low opportunity.

If one thinks about opportunity as the predicate, a starting point, where a president facing, for example, high public demand for action, with large partisan majorities in both houses of Congress, in the aftermath of a landslide electoral victory, one might conclude that the president has clout. One expects a great deal of success in such circumstances. That is where skill and experience come into play. A highly skilled president in a high-opportunity setting (e.g., FDR after the 1932 elections when the country was facing a depression) is likely to achieve success. By contrast, a low-opportunity president with limited skill and experience is likely to do poorly. Opportunity and skill—that is the secret sauce of effective presidential leadership.

A STORY

Presidents have a notoriously difficult time achieving passage of their domestic agendas, especially after year one of their presidency. Year one tends to be the most fruitful time for presidents, who are fresh off an electoral success, as Congress may be more receptive to the will of the people and the pressures of the president. As Lyndon Johnson noted, "You've got to give it all you can that first year. Doesn't matter what kind of a majority you come in with. You've got just one year when they treat you right."[11]

This "first year phenomenon" is not unique to the United States. New administrations, regardless of regime type,[12] that can get off to a good start and "hit the ground running"[13] often achieve a level of political success unmatched in later years of a term in office.

The early days of the Biden administration bear this out. Not only was Joe Biden active in issuing a series of executive orders, but he was able, within the first few months of his term, to pass a massive $1.9 trillion stimulus bill. In the first year of a new administration, Democratic presidents tend to propose a major social welfare program while Republican presidents usually propose a large tax cut. Biden, a Democrat, proposed The American Rescue Plan, a program on a scale surprisingly large even for a Democrat. And he did so at a time of economic distress and soaring federal deficits.

The Biden relief package included direct relief to individuals hurt by the COVID-caused economic downturn, extensions of unemployment benefits, an expansion of the food stamps program, relief for renters in jeopardy of being evicted, direct subsidies to hard-pressed state and local governments, health-care subsidies, and expanded child-care benefits. It was estimated that the child-care benefits alone would cut child poverty in half.

How did Biden accomplish all this in so short a time? Biden entered office with a very high level of experience, demonstrated drive, determination, and a significant level of skill, faced a Congress (barely) under the control of his party, and took advantage of public demand for action. And do not forget the circumstances on the ground that Biden confronted: an economic recession caused by the pandemic. This crisis opened a door to power for Biden.

But it wasn't long before the forces of inertia took hold, and Biden was met by an intransigent Congress. Step one was successful, but the opposition forces in Congress quickly put up roadblocks, and Biden was met not only with pushback from Republicans in Congress but also by conflicts between the moderate and progressive wings of his own party. The Republicans wanted "nothing"; the moderates wanted "some"; the progressives wanted "all of it." And President Biden was left trying to herd the cats in Congress.

Theodore Roosevelt famously lamented, "If I only could be President and Congress, too, just for ten minutes . . ." Presidents are not kings, they are not dictators, they are but one part of a three-branch government (cynics would say it is a three-ring circus). They can't govern alone. And they have a hard time governing within a checks-and-balances system that separates and shares power.

MY VIEW

This analysis still begs the question: Which is more important, skill or opportunity? The answer, of course, is "both." While a bit of a cop-out, actually this view does capture the essence of the problem of presidential leadership in a separated system. High skill levels always help, but skill alone will not get one very far. Skill with opportunity (and resources) can and often does lead to high levels of achievement. Low levels of skill and low levels of opportunity will only rarely be converted into success.[14]

In my own estimation, there is a hierarchy of factors that contribute to presidential success (table 5.2). In this hierarchy, as one can see, factors relating to opportunity dominate. But there are also several key skills a successful president must have.

Presidents can be FDR-like if the political stars align. But this rarely happens. Thus, our high expectations inevitably lead to—except in a few cases—disappointment. Are our expectations too high? Should we be more understanding of the limits of presidential leadership? Yes. Will we be more understanding? Almost certainly, no.

The case of Lyndon Johnson is instructive. Johnson became president after the tragic 1963 assassination of John F. Kennedy. Johnson's vast legislative experience, strategic sense, guile, persuasive skills, plus majorities in both houses of Congress all

TABLE 5.2 HIERARCHY OF SUCCESS FACTORS

Success factor	Opportunity or skill?
A significant party majority in Congress	Opportunity
In crisis times	Opportunity
In foreign policy	Opportunity
When there is high public demand	Opportunity
Wide-ranging experience	Skill
Sound judgment	Skill
Managerial adroitness	Skill
Communicator capabilities	Skill

contributed to his success with Congress. In the eighty-seventh Congress (1961–1963), the Democrats had a 64–36 seat margin in the Senate and a 262–175 seat margin in the House. In the eighty-eighth Congress (1963–1965), the Democrats enjoyed a 67–33 seat margin in the Senate and a 258–186 seat margin in the House. And in the eighty-ninth Congress (1965–1967), the Democrats held a 68–32 seat margin in the Senate and a 295–140 seat margin in the House. Do the math. Johnson could lose a dozen votes in the Senate and sixty in the House and still win. That is a level of political opportunity that really matters.

And what was the payoff? The eighty-ninth Congress passed legislation establishing Medicare, Medicaid, the Department of Transportation, the Department of Housing and Urban Development, and the National Endowment for the Humanities. Congress also increased the federal minimum wage, passed the Higher Education Act, and provided federal aid to elementary and secondary education. It passed the Water Quality Act, the Motor Vehicle Air Pollution Control Act, the Highway and Motor Vehicle Safety Acts, the Demonstration Cities Act, the Clean Waters Restoration Act, the Fair Packaging and Labeling Act, and a significant amendment to the Immigration and Nationality Act.

Yes, Johnson was a legislative master, but he was dealt three aces and parlayed that hand into one of the most successful legislative achievements in history. Skill *and* opportunity.

CONCLUSION

Skill converts opportunities into power and accomplishment. High skill and high opportunity—such as when FDR became president in 1933—can lead to dramatic policy changes. Low skill and low opportunity result in political failure (figure 5.1).

	Skill	
	High	Low
Opportunity High	Franklin D. Roosevelt Lyndon Johnson	George W. Bush Ronald Reagan
Opportunity Low	Theodore Roosevelt Bill Clinton Barack Obama George H. W. Bush	Gerald Ford Jimmy Carter Donald Trump

FIGURE 5.1 Skill versus opportunity

From this we can determine which presidents are overachievers and which are underachievers. We would expect presidents in quadrant one to be high achievers, and FDR certainly was. Presidents in quadrant two (high in skill, low in opportunity) must work hard for more modest success. Presidents such as Theodore Roosevelt and Barack Obama can be seen as overachievers, while Bill Clinton and George H. W. Bush performed roughly as expected.

Presidents with low skill and high opportunity (quadrant three) tend to disappoint. They have the opportunity to lead, but a lack of skill betrays them (George W. Bush). We should not expect much of presidents in quadrant four, low skill and low opportunity, and the three presidents listed are all considered as low achievers or failures.

6

WILL THE FUTURE OF THE U.S. PRESIDENCY BE ONE OF LIBERAL DEMOCRACY OR ILLIBERAL DEMOCRACY?

H as liberal democracy run its course? And if so, what is likely to replace it? Today, liberal democracies across the globe are under attack and on the defensive. Many citizens believe their governments serve elites, do not represent their interests, and are corrupt and ineffective. A populist rebellion against the status quo pits those who defend liberal governments against a rising tide of illiberal voters who demand that their governments represent their interests against the status quo establishment elites. They want a strong leader to tear down the old sclerotic system (referred to as "the swamp" by Donald Trump) and "get things done."

Of course, liberal democracies have been under attack before (U.S. Civil War), but today's rebellion is the most serious challenge to the status quo for the past one hundred sixty years. The old order (largely white and male) is giving way to a more diverse citizenry (Hispanic and Black), and the loss of white status domination has created a reaction in which many of those who feel their status threatened turn their backs on liberal democracy and call for a savior to rescue them. It is a battle over not only *who* will govern but *how* they are to govern.

In 1787, the form of government established by the American framers, a *liberal democracy*, was the new challenge to the status quo of kings and aristocratic rule. The myth of the divine right of kings was being challenged by what historian Edmund S. Morgan referred to as the divine right of the people.[1] The old order that had reigned supreme for many years was threatened by a unique set of ideas percolating largely from the bottom up (the growing demands of the people) but also from the top down via influential political philosophers who emerged from the Enlightenment (the age of reason) to promote democratic aspirations.

Taking their historical cue not from Athenian democracy of the age of Pericles but from the Roman Republic (pre-Caesar), a growing chorus began touting the dangers of hereditary monopolies and celebrated government by consent of the people, a set system of laws and rules, and limitation on the scope and authority of government.

In our age of globalization and hyperchange, should the United States be governed by a *liberal democracy* or would we be better served with an *illiberal democracy*?

The United States is a modern superpower, yet we are still governed by rules and structures invented more than 235 years ago. An eighteenth-century constitution is guiding a twenty-first-century superpower. Have we outgrown the Constitution of 1787, and do we need to modernize and streamline our system of government? After all, the coat that fit you when you were ten years old has stayed the same size, but you haven't—you've grown, changed, and the coat that fit you years ago would be ridiculously small on you now. Can much of the same be said about our Constitution? Does it establish a leadership institution, a president, that may have been appropriate in 1787, 1840, or 1900 but is today an impediment to good governing?

THE PROBLEM CLEARLY DEFINED

The post–Cold War era (1989 to today) and the implosion of the Soviet Union led to the embrace of liberal democracies across the globe, leading some to celebrate the rise of democracy and the end of history.[2] But the celebration was short lived. By the 2010s, liberal democracies seemed tired and spent, and with globalization and hyperchange, governments seemed unable to meet the demands of citizens. A populist backlash against the perceived shortcoming of liberal democracies led to the rise of illiberal democracies across the globe, in which strong leaders were to overcome the limitations of the tired old democracy and provide strong, decisive leadership. Too strong, perhaps.

But illiberal democracies present their own problems. Does the rise of illiberal democracy spell doom for liberal democracies, and what might be the implications of this trend for the United States and democracies across the globe?

WHY DOES THIS MATTER?

Today, across the globe, democracy is under assault; and the United States runs the risk that its 235-year experiment with liberal democracy is in jeopardy. If the United States embraces illiberal democracy, it would be a radical break from the status quo system that has guided us since 1789. Our rule-of-law system, which is based on individual rights and limited government, would be in jeopardy, and we would risk coming full circle from a hereditary monarch (rule by the king of England) to an electoral monarch (rule by a single strong leader).

Today, the status quo (and the "enemy" to some) is the liberal democratic orthodoxy that to its critics is too slow and unresponsive, captured by the elites, and not responsive to the needs or will of the people. What was once (1780s) the solution to our problems (centralized, tyrannical rule) is now seen by some as the problem to be solved.

THE QUESTION CLEARLY POSED

Liberal democracy with a circumscribed presidency is being challenged by illiberal forces that hope to unleash the presidency from the restrictions of the Constitution. What might we gain or lose if illiberal democracy replaces liberal democracy in the United States?

THE FUTURE OF THE PRESIDENCY

If liberal democracy is the status quo, what is the challenge? Illiberal democracy. Liberal democracies are characterized by representative rule that is based on constitutions and the rule of law, with limited government, individual rights, and checks and balances on leaders. Illiberal democracies[3] hold elections to elect strongmen to govern, sweeping away checks and balances and the limits on their rule. These strongmen are elected (thus the term "democracies"), but illiberal governments do not recognize or impose the checks associated with liberal democracies (thus they are "illiberal").

In Russia, Vladimir Putin (while popular and popularly elected) exercises a brand of heavy-handed control that stifles freedom all in the name of the new (or old) Russia. Witness also the leadership shifts in Turkey, Hungary, Poland, the Philippines, and elsewhere.

Putin in Russia and Xi in China offer two alternative models to that of liberal democracy. Putin's "winner-take-all" brand of democratic authoritarianism offers a brand of leadership, of "star power" some find quite appealing.[4]

The battle between liberal and illiberal notions of democracy and leadership is stark and consequential. American notions of political leadership that are grounded in age of reason/Enlightenment assumptions are being challenged in the age of globalization and hyperchange. Citizens and voters throughout the West believe that their governments serve only society's elites, have left average citizens out, and do not serve their needs or represent their interests.

A period characterized by angry voters who display insurgent, antigovernment, anti-establishment sentiments presents a stark contrast between the liberal forces of the status quo and the demands of voters who see their governments as not serving and representing "us." Populist movements have challenged the established order[5] and threaten regime change in several countries.[6] Anti-immigrant, anti-elitist, and anti-diversity forces are on the rise, and liberal governments are on the defensive. Outsiders, Trump in the United States and Le Pen in France, once seen as unelectable, are now closing in on power.[7]

This has led to a growing belief that the old order should be shattered, as it is too slow to move, too supportive of cosmopolitanism, and too skewed toward "them." In France, the United States, the United Kingdom, and elsewhere, voters want to "take back their countries."

The immediate cause of this may be the aftermath of the 2007 economic slump and its slow and uneven recovery, the growing economic inequality, plus stagnant economies and stagnant wages, but the real culprits are *globalization* and *hyperchange.*

Liberal governments have not and perhaps cannot respond quickly or forcefully enough to the forces unleashed by globalization and hyperchange. Angry and impatient for results, voters choose the illiberal alternative, electing strongmen who can lead with authority.

Another way to look at the liberal versus illiberal leadership debate is to reformulate the categories as more "democratic" (liberal democracy) and more "autocratic" (illiberal). The Polity IV index by the Center for Systemic Peace has done the heavy lifting for us in this regard. Each year the center provides both a democracy and an autocracy index. The democracy index is rated from zero to ten and is based on three key factors:

> One is the presence of institutions and procedures through which citizens can express effective preferences about alternative policies and leaders. Second is the existence of institutionalized constraints on the exercise of power by the executive. Third is the guarantee of civil liberties to all citizens in their daily lives and in acts of political participation.[8]

By contrast, the autocracy index focuses on the absence of robust political competition:

> In mature form, autocracies sharply restrict or suppress competitive political participation. Their chief executives are chosen in a regularized process of selection within the political elite, and once in office they exercise power with few institutional constraints. Most modern autocracies also exercise a high degree of directiveness over social and economic activity, but we regard this as a function of political ideology and choice, not a defining property of autocracy.[9]

As defined by the Polity IV index, liberal democratic leaders are fully subject to the "democratic" requirements of having avenues through which citizens can choose (regular free elections), living under institutionalized constraints (separation of powers), and guarantees of civil liberties to all citizens. Autocratic regimes lack some of the features. They may have elections, but institutional restraints are weak, and citizen rights may be in jeopardy. And while the illiberal brand of leadership may not conform to all the autocratic standards, it does tend in that direction.

The promise of the leaders as saviors becomes appealing. The model? Identify the enemy (immigrants, or a governmental weakness, or cosmopolitanism), bring in the savior, and throw out the status quo. In this context, Putanism (a strong leader riding on the shoulders of the people, blaming "them" for our troubles) becomes the go-to option.

Consider the rising tide of nonliberal leadership abroad in the West. That the Putanist model has become so popular is testimony to the perceived failure or weakness of liberal governments throughout the West (table 6.1).

TABLE 6.1 NONLIBERAL LEADERSHIP ABROAD IN THE WEST

Country	Party leader	Party
Austria	Norbert Hofer	Freedom Party
Czech Republic	Andrej Babis	Action of Dissatisfied Citizens Party (ANO)
France	Marine Le Pen	National Rally
Germany	Frauke Petry	Alternative für Deutschland (AFD)
Hungary	Viktor Orbán	Fidesz
The Netherlands	Geert Wilders	Party of Freedom
The Philippines	Rodrigo Duterte	PDP-Laban
Poland	Jarosław Kaczyński	Law and Justice
Russia	Vladimir Putin	United Russia
Turkey	Recep Tayyip Erdoğan	Justice and Development
United Kingdom	Nigel Farage	UK Independence Party (UKIP)
United States	Donald Trump	(Tea Party) Republican
Venezuela	Hugo Chavez	United Socialist Party of Venezuela

Some argue that China's rise economically is the model for the future: economic capitalism in a market economy merged with a strong, centralized command state. Or, more likely, a Putanist strongman as a modern-day Leviathan.

Deadlocked democracies, ineffective governments—the perceived failure of liberal democracy—this gives rise to a robust form of "democratic" leadership sans checks and balances and the rule of law. If limited government is the enemy, give the leaders power. But such a step is both a governing philosophy and prescription for action that makes societies vulnerable to the vagaries of personal power.

LOSING MY RELIGION, OR THE DECLINE OF DEMOCRATIC FAITH

That's me in the corner
That's me in the spotlight
Losing my religion

—REM, "LOSING MY RELIGION"

The numbers are clear and concerning—at least to those who value liberal democracy and hope to strengthen and grow democracies across the globe. Overall support for liberal democracy is in decline, the threat of autocratic or illiberal democracy is on the rise,[10] and populist forces increasingly see Western or liberal democracies as a problem to be solved, not as a solution to their problems.[11]

Breaking faith may, in some ways, be a national response to the decline in middle-class fortune. After all, workers were hit hard by the 2007 recession, and as the economy recovered, the benefit seemed to go to the upper class while working-class wages were stagnant. The reality of the rich getting richer and the poor and the middle class facing stagnation led to the rise of a populist revolt on the left (Bernie Sanders and the Occupy movement) and on the right (Donald Trump and the Tea Party). The legitimate anxiety and fears of citizens may have been exploited by ambitious politicians, but their concerns were real. With neither political party addressing their grievances, faith in the system eroded.[12]

Regarding the apparent fragility of the public's commitment to democracy, it should be remembered that for most of human history, democracy held little sway with elite and general audiences. From Plato on, the case for democracy only became viable in the eighteenth century, and the much vaunted (though premature) announcement of the victory of democracy over all other forms of government[13] occurred only after the fall of the Berlin Wall in 1989.

If democracy has long had its critics, in the 1990s it became the gold standard for governments across the globe. And yet, challenges to the current orthodoxy present[14] opportunities for making the case for either democratic caution[15] ("too much democracy can be a bad thing") or for a more limited version of democracy in an age of globalization (illiberal democracy).[16]

A Pew survey of thirty-eight nations found widespread support for either representative or direct democracy (figure 6.1), but also noted

a deepening anxiety about the future of democracy around the world has spread over the last few years. Emboldened autocrats and raising populists have shaken assumptions about the future trajectory of liberal democracy. . . . Scholars have documented a global democratic recession, and some now warn that even long-established "consolidated" democracy can slip toward more authoritarian politics.[17]

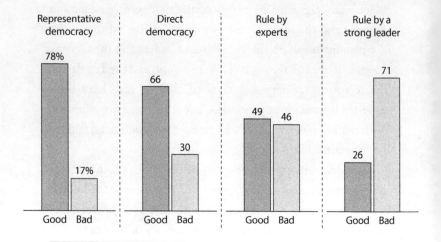

FIGURE 6.1 Widespread support for representative and direct democracy exists, but many people are also open to nondemocratic alternatives

Source: Richard Wike, Katie Simmons, Bruce Stokes, and Janell Fetterolf, "Globally, Broad Support for Representative and Direct Democracy," Pew Research Center, October 16, 2017, https://www.pewresearch.org/global/2017/10/16/globally -broad-support-for-representative-and-direct-democracy/.

The Pew report also warns of the rise and support for strong (illiberal) executive power. The report notes that while support for autocracy is low, many voters are willing to entertain certain nondemocratic forms of governing (figure 6.2).

Much of the suspicion of democratic forms stems from the decline of "trust" in government. Where trust is low, support for democracy declines (figure 6.3).[18]

Yascha Mounk and Roberto Foa take a more alarming view of democracy's place in our world and argue: "Public attitudes towards democracy, we show, have soured over time. Citizens, especially millennials, have lost faith in the democratic system. They are more likely to express hostile views of democracy. And they vote for anti-establishment parties and candidates that disregard long-standing democratic norms in ever greater numbers."[19]

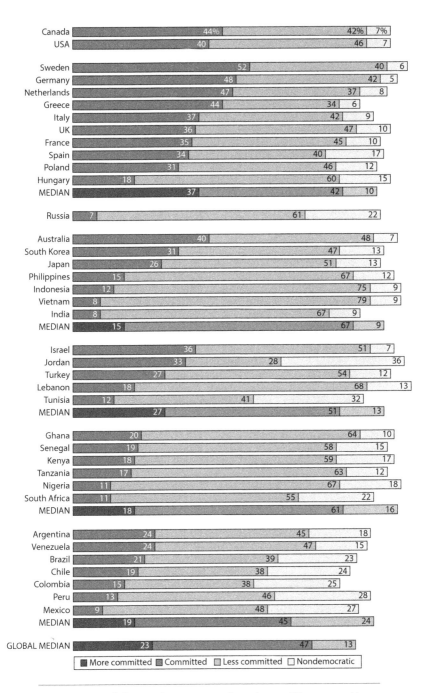

	More committed	Committed	Less committed	Nondemocratic
Canada		44%	42%	7%
USA		40	46	7
Sweden		52	40	6
Germany		48	42	5
Netherlands		47	37	8
Greece		44	34	6
Italy		37	42	9
UK		36	47	10
France		35	45	10
Spain		34	40	17
Poland		31	46	12
Hungary		18	60	15
MEDIAN		37	42	10
Russia		7	61	22
Australia		40	48	7
South Korea		31	47	13
Japan		26	51	13
Philippines		15	67	12
Indonesia		12	75	9
Vietnam		8	79	9
India		8	67	9
MEDIAN		15	67	9
Israel		36	51	7
Jordan		33	28	36
Turkey		27	54	12
Lebanon		18	68	13
Tunisia		12	41	32
MEDIAN		27	51	13
Ghana		20	64	10
Senegal		19	58	15
Kenya		18	59	17
Tanzania		17	63	12
Nigeria		11	67	18
South Africa		11	55	22
MEDIAN		18	61	16
Argentina		24	45	18
Venezuela		24	47	15
Brazil		21	39	23
Chile		19	38	24
Colombia		15	38	25
Peru		13	46	28
Mexico		9	48	27
MEDIAN		19	45	24
GLOBAL MEDIAN		23	47	13

■ More committed ■ Committed ☐ Less committed ☐ Nondemocratic

FIGURE 6.2 Substantial percentages of people are willing to consider nondemocratic options

Source: Richard Wike, Katie Simmons, Bruce Stokes, and Janell Fetterolf, "Globally, Broad Support for Representative and Direct Democracy," Pew Research Center, October 16, 2017, https://www.pewresearch.org/global/2017/10/16/globally -broad-support-for-representative-and-direct-democracy/.

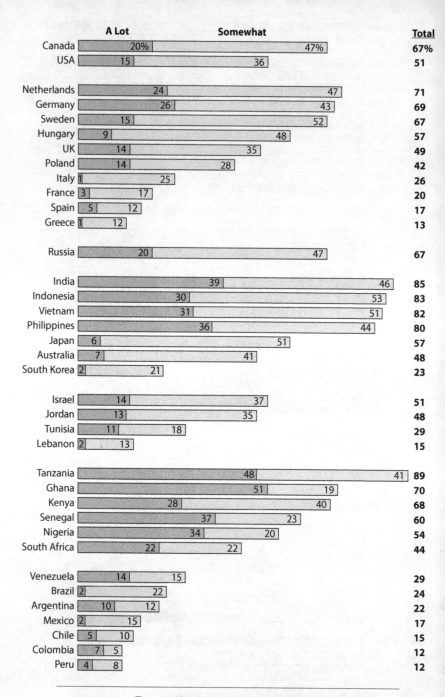

	A Lot	Somewhat	Total
Canada	20%	47%	67%
USA	15	36	51
Netherlands	24	47	71
Germany	26	43	69
Sweden	15	52	67
Hungary	9	48	57
UK	14	35	49
Poland	14	28	42
Italy	1	25	26
France	3	17	20
Spain	5	12	17
Greece	1	12	13
Russia	20	47	67
India	39	46	85
Indonesia	30	53	83
Vietnam	31	51	82
Philippines	36	44	80
Japan	6	51	57
Australia	7	41	48
South Korea	2	21	23
Israel	14	37	51
Jordan	13	35	48
Tunisia	11	18	29
Lebanon	2	13	15
Tanzania	48	41	89
Ghana	51	19	70
Kenya	28	40	68
Senegal	37	23	60
Nigeria	34	20	54
South Africa	22	22	44
Venezuela	14	15	29
Brazil	2	22	24
Argentina	10	12	22
Mexico	2	15	17
Chile	5	10	15
Colombia	7	5	12
Peru	4	8	12

FIGURE 6.3 Few worldwide have a lot of trust in their government

Source: Richard Wike, Katie Simmons, Bruce Stokes, and Janell Fetterolf, "Globally, Broad Support for Representative and Direct Democracy," Pew Research Center, October 16, 2017, https://www.pewresearch.org/global/2017/10/16/globally -broad-support-for-representative-and-direct-democracy/.

Voters in the United States do not have a high level of "confidence" that their governing institutions are working on their behalf. Roughly, one in three have a "great deal" or "quite a lot" of confidence in the Supreme Court and presidency, and a shocking 9 percent have confidence in Congress (table 6.2). How can a government expect to govern when confidence in that government—its legitimacy, perhaps—is too low? And is it a chicken or egg phenomenon: Does low confidence cause government to break down or does breakdown cause a loss of confidence? Either way, these numbers (as does the standard of "trust" question; figures 6.4 and 6.5) suggest that governmental legitimacy is in jeopardy.[20]

TABLE 6.2 AMERICANS' CONFIDENCE IN U.S. INSTITUTIONS, 2019

	A great deal / Quite a lot (%)	Some (%)	Very little / None (%)	Net confidence (%)
The military	73	18	8	+65
Small business	68	24	8	+60
The police	53	31	17	+36
The presidency	38	17	44	−6
The U.S. Supreme Court	38	40	21	+17
The church or organized religion	36	36	29	+7
The medical system	36	38	26	+10
Banks	30	43	26	+4
Public schools	29	42	29	0
Organized labor	29	45	24	+5
The criminal justice system	24	40	36	−12
Newspapers	23	37	39	−16
Big business	23	41	34	−11
Television news	18	33	48	−30
Congress	11	36	52	−41

Source: "Americans' Confidence in Institution Stays Low." *Gallup*, June 13, 2019.
Note: Net confidence = A great deal / Quite a lot minus Very little / None (vol.); (vol.) = volunteered response.

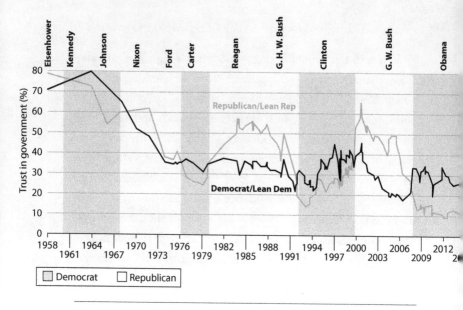

FIGURE 6.4 Trust in government by party, 1958–2015

Source: Pew Research Center, "Beyond Distrust: How Americans View Their Government," November 23, 2015, https://www.pewresearch.org/politics/2015/11/23/beyond-distrust-how-americans-view-their-government/.

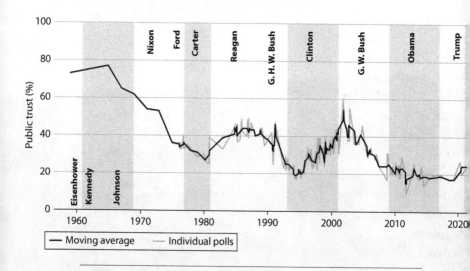

FIGURE 6.5 Public trust in government is near historic lows

Source: Pew Research Center, "Public Trust in Government: 1958–2021," May 17, 2021, https://www.pewresearch.org/politics/2021/05/17/public-trust-in-government-1958-2021/.

Alarm about the state of democracy is reflected in the voices of scholars, practitioners, and citizens. Such alarm is grounded in both anecdote and evidence. Data compiled by Yascha Mounk reveals that nearly one in four millennials believes that democracy is a bad way to run a country. And young voters increasingly think that a political system with a strong leader whose power was not impeded by Congress or even elections was a good or very good idea. Roughly one in six favored military rule.[21]

DEMOCRACY—AN IDEA IN DISPUTE

"Democracy" can mean many things to many people. Some political scientists advocate a "procedurally minimalist" view that includes:

- Free, fair, open competitive elections.
- Universal adult suffrage.
- Guaranteed individual rights, such as speech, press, and assembly.

"Liberal democracy" would add:

- Limited government.
- Rule-of-law regime.
- Some form of checks and balances.

Democracies, it seems—at least the liberal variety—are in retreat across the globe. While the number of democracies increased in the 1980s and 1990s, in the past decade many robust liberal democracies have morphed into illiberal forms of democracy, and the foundations of democracy of all types face challenges. Can democracies maintain the level of public support necessary to fend off all of these challenges?[22]

In a way, the rise of illiberal democracy over liberal democracy may be seen as a victory of Thomas Hobbes over John Locke, and Jean-Jacques Rousseau over Edmund Burke. Hobbes saw a world of violence (life outside of society was, to Hobbes, "nasty, brutish, and short") where a strong government was needed to create order out of chaos. Rousseau, more optimistic about humans in the state of nature is seen today by many as the "enabler of democratic dictatorship,"[23] or what he called "the general will." Both Hobbes and Rousseau—who disagree on many things—agree that a strong leader is desirable. For Rousseau, it was leadership embodied in the "general will." For Hobbes, it was Leviathan. John Locke is an advocate of liberal democracy and the defender of a form of "liberal conservatism."[24] Both Hobbes and Locke would defend the liberal democratic model under discussion here.

The West's growing democratic distemper. Western democracies are increasingly plagued by a contagion of anger, fear, and political backlash. The middle class, often seen as a backbone of stability for societies, is threatening to turn against established liberal democracy and embrace a form of illiberal democracy as a solution to the perceived troubles. No democracy seems immune. Increasingly, voters are becoming alienated, turning against established orders, and reaching out in search of a savior to lead them out of this malaise. They seem to believe that governments no longer serve their interest, and they are "mad as hell and not going to take it." Uncertainty and disaffection, resentment and insecurity are spreading in Western democracies as the glue that once bound us together is losing its adhesive qualities.

The growing anger is largely the result of globalization and rapid-fire change, monumental changes that have left a crisis of governability as weak governments grope for effective responses. This creates a widening gap between what voters want and what governments are capable of delivering. It is no secret why this gap exists: governments no longer have the capacity to direct policy outcomes as they once did. Forces such as the "market" and technology, interdependence and interconnectedness conspire against governmental control, and governments no longer serve the needs or interest of people, fail to deliver on promises, or are incompetent.

Leaders are unable to satisfy these demands because a considerable amount of power has slipped through their hands. Decisions no longer rest with a nation-state but must be painstakingly agreed to by multiple actors in government and the private sector. Leaders are weaker as power has to be shared with new claimants: the force of the market, developing nations, regional powers, religious groups, tribal loyalties, and technological change. Leaders are now dealmakers, negotiators, facilitators, agenda setters, multilateral conveners. Our image of the bold leader courageously charting a new course, who through sheer force of will achieves great results (the "great man theory"), has given way to the meeting-caller and the consensus builder—not a very romantic image of leadership, but one that fits the current reality.

The Economist went so far to assert that "a spectre is haunting the rich world. It is the spectre of ungovernability" and warned that "opinion polls everywhere show increasing numbers of people losing patience with democratic niceties and hankering after a strong man."[25]

WHO IS THREATENING THE OLD ORDER?

Most of the revolt against established leaders comes from the middle and working classes. These people tend to be white, male, less educated, blue-collar workers who feel threatened by globalization and changes in their societies. Their angst has found a populist movement that tends to at times lean toward the xenophobic; it is largely nationalist, is antigovernment and anti-establishment, is usually anti-immigrant, and often anti-elitist. As *The Economist* noted, "support for xenophobic populism is strongest among those who are older, non-university educated, working class, white and male." They are Donald Trump's "silent majority" and Marine Le Pen's "forgotten people." The result is a surge in angry voters, a decline in political and social stability, and a move to the political right.

These voters fear what the future may hold. They are anxious and afraid about losing their social position and status. Many feel vulnerable to the rapid-fire changes going on around them. There are forces at work that they can neither understand nor control. Their jobs seem threatened by outsourcing or immigrants. Their wages are stagnant, and they are economically marginalized. They see their societies changing, with people of different origins, colors, and religions "taking over." They continue to fear the threats posed by terrorism and do not see the government doing enough to protect them. And they feel powerless to change things.

The result is a steep decline in trust of government, an antigovernment, anti-immigrant surge, a revolt against the establishment and its governing elites. They feel that the world is passing them by, and politicians are too weak or corrupt to fight for their interests. The "lamestream media" is merely a tool of governing elites and does not represent them or speak to their needs. The plutocrats, the donor class, the politicians, and the hordes of immigrants are the enemy. They are in a battle for the soul of the nation. And there is no shortage of would-be saviors who are all too willing to stoke the embers of fear.

All Western democracies are to varying degrees facing this revolt. In the United States, a symptom is Donald Trump. But the root causes are deeper than merely Trump. In January 2016, more than 50 percent of all likely Republican voters supported an outsider or hard-right candidate for president. To be an establishment candidate was a mark of shame, they quickly found out. Donald Trump's immigrant bashing, anti-Muslim statements, and generally derogatory tone, something we would've laughed at twenty years ago, now end in applause an adoration. In fact, the more anger-fueled Trump's message, the more he garnered support.

In France, the far-right, neo-Nazi National Rally, led by Marine Le Pen, did well in early voting in the 2015 elections, but after it was clear that her party might win seats in the legislature, the more mainstream parties worked together to head off the rise of the National Rally candidates. Le Pen's anti-immigrant hostility, made more credible during the Syrian refugee crisis, was represented by the motto, "France for the French."

In Hungary, led by Prime Minister Viktor Orbán, a self-consciously illiberal state is developing, with Vladimir Putin as role model.[26] Likewise, in Poland, Jarosław Kaczyński, of the Law and Justice Party, is quickly becoming the poster child of illiberal, Putin-style democracy. Even in Great Britain, anti-immigrant and anti-European Union sentiment, at first the key issue for the United Kingdom Independence Party (UKIP), pressed Conservative prime minister David Cameron to allow a "Brexit" vote from the European Union. Russia, of course, is the role model for illiberal government. But even in northern Europe, Sweden, the Netherlands, and Denmark—once firmly established liberal bastions—are swinging more to the right. All these nations are being animated by anti-immigrant, anti-elite, sometimes racist, nativist, and populist sentiments, and all are being drawn into the rise of "strongmen" and the emergence of illiberal democracy.

WHAT DO THEY WANT?

"I want it to stop"—they want to reverse history and go back to a time when they were in control, when it was their country, and the "others" were a random annoyance, but not a major threat. They want to restore and reinvigorate old national identities against the threat of a watered-down culture. They feel vulnerable and want to feel secure. So, they search for a savior to rescue them.

The governing frustrations of the Trump presidency reflect the conflict between "liberal institutions" (e.g., Congress, the courts, the media) and the illiberal tendencies of President Trump. Frustrated by the checks and balances that challenged him, and incredulous that the law limited his policy-making options, Trump—often via early morning tweets—attacked "the system" (sometimes disparagingly referred to as "the deep state") as he tried to free himself of the system's limits. Trump's frustrations reflect a victory for the sources of liberal democracy against the personalization of illiberal leadership.

THE AGE OF IMPERIAL EXECUTIVE

Because of these changes, the age of the imperial executive is upon us. Across the globe, executives rise as legislatures decline in power. "Presidentialism" is increasingly seen as the problem we need to solve in the twenty-first century.

The rise of illiberal leaders suggests a disturbing trend: as democratic distemper spreads across the world's democracies, the people, angry and fearful, look to a strongman—a savior—who can lead them out of the darkness and into (or back to) a safe, secure, and bright future.

With the collapse of the Soviet Union, the West began to celebrate its victory over the forces of "evil" as a great threat was smashed and democracy rose triumphant. It was, in Francis Fukuyama's premature phrase, "the end of history." A democratic wave swept across the former Soviet Republics, and the world went from about sixteen democracies in 1987 to more than one hundred twenty in 2010. We had finally made the world safe for democracy. Or had we?

Fukuyama was writing at a heady time for democracy and the West.

On January 29, 1991, speaking to a joint session of Congress, President George H. W. Bush described "a New World order, where diverse nations are drawn together in common cause to achieve the universal aspirations of mankind—peace and security, freedom and the rule of law." He praised "the triumph of democratic ideas in eastern Europe and Latin America." Less than a year later, on December 26, 1991, the Soviet Union disappeared *entirely*; in its place stood fifteen nascent democracies.

The executive is a truly "modern" institution. It is built for speed. Executives have an impressive adaptation capability, as only one person needs to decide, and the institution (normally) follows. Executives can act, preempt others, and set the stage and tone of action. They can move quickly to wherever it is necessary or desirable.

Legislatures, on the other hand, are slow and deliberative bodies. They are built on bargaining, compromise, and deal making. There are multiple veto points in the legislative process. They face an adaptation crisis. Often, they are forced to react to an executive act. Legislatures were built for a quieter, slower time. They are eighteenth-century institutions operating in the twenty-first century.

The danger we face today is that liberal democracies are morphing into illiberal democracies, and with a centralization of power in the hands of one person, the risk of a Putinist-style democracy looms large. A strong leader armed with the support of the people can sweep away checks and balances and act boldly, governing in the name of the people. And who is to stop this imperial executive?

That is the return of the *Goldilocks dilemma*: this executive is too hot, this one too cold. We can't seem to get it just right. As liberal democracies fail to adequately respond to and solve the problems they face, the people grow angry and begin to demand bold solutions. Forget about the checks on power, we demand the exercise of power. And if that means ruffling a few constitutional feathers, so be it. But if liberal democracies are too cold, illiberal democracies are often too hot.

If liberal democracies restrain power, illiberal democracies unleash it. It is tempting to demand that the executive be given commensurate power to meet the demands of our times. But the risk exceeds the rewards. An executive unhinged is an executive to be feared. Can the liberal democracies withstand this onslaught?

Was it the success of liberal democracy that also planted the seeds of its own destruction? Or as R. R. Palmer wrote, "the revolution of the west had created the tools for the ongoing revolution against the west."[27] Is there, then, no "end of history," merely stages, twists and turns, growth and decline, with no clear trajectory toward liberal democracy? It seems presumptuous to assume that *we have found the answer* and should not rest on our laurels and demand that the globe embraces *our* system.

IS THERE A WAY OUT?

Political scientists Stephen Levitsky and Daniel Ziblatt argue that one of the key indicators of democratic danger is when a system's "guardrails"—the rule of law, civility, the acceptance of election outcomes, adherence to norms, tolerance, fair-fighting, etc.—weaken or evaporate. The formal (laws) and the informal (behavior) matter. While populists decry the dangers posed by immigration, the "real" threat to democratic stability is not new arrivals, but homegrown radicals and terrorists. The January 6, 2021, insurrection is a footnote in a larger decline in civility and a rise in right-wing violence. When "facts" become unhinged from evidence, when sincerity replaces evidence, when intensity of belief supplants facts, and when one sees political rivals as existential threats, it excuses any and all efforts to save yourself from the perceived ravages of the opposition. If "they" are pure evil, any means necessary to stop them is acceptable. The rule of law gives way to the rule of the angry mob.[28]

Effective governance would help diminish the appeal of anti-democratic faces, as would a positive message and a new governing coalition. A more equitable spread of wealth from the economic recovery would be a positive step, as would a more coordinated and robust response to terrorism. But mostly we need a reasoned defense of liberal democracy—its ideas and ideals, its benefits and contributions. We must also deal with those complaints and fears that may be legitimate and real. Yes, our middle-class wages are stagnant; yes, terrorism is an ongoing concern; yes, demographic changes are changing the face of the nation. But if *bridge* builders are to reclaim the support of voters, they must offer a better alternative than those offered by *wall* builders.

The rise of illiberal democracy threatens to undermine the governments of the West. In troubled and troubling times, it is understandable that these democracies will be under fire. But sometimes the worst of times brings out the worst in us. The West must offer a better alternative. It must define a new narrative for the disillusioned public. We know what the angry voters are against. Now we need to give them something to be positive for.

In this post-heroic age, can leaders govern?[29] The list of impediments to presidential power is already long: separation of powers, structural roadblocks, unreasonably high public expectations, and so on. Now, add to this list the constraints placed on the presidency in an age of hyperchange and globalization. If things were not already tough, a president now faces increased demands and diminished resources. Things have gotten worse at home, with hyper-partisanship creating an end to compromise, let alone the "water's edge" foreign policy myth.

A STORY

It was 2010, and the Tea Party movement was just beginning to spread. A protest coalition of white working-class conservatives, libertarians, disgruntled Republicans, and a sprinkle of white supremacists, the Tea Party protesters were against what they saw as excessive taxes, the elites who they maintained controlled the government for their own benefit and to the detriment of everyday Americans, excessive government rules and regulations, illegal immigrants, and the rise of people of color.

Upset that the government was meddling in the affairs of individuals and thwarting liberty, Tea Party advocates began to protest against the status quo. In an ironic twist, one protester sported a banner that read "GOVERNMENT, KEEP YOUR HANDS OFF MY MEDICARE"; the irony of course being that Medicare *is* a government program.

To the Tea Party, the "establishment" was the enemy. Elites were sucking all of society's profits and resources and stuffing them into their pockets while "the people" struggled to make ends meet. This populist rebellion, aligned with though not always supportive of the Republican Party, demanded change. Just what they wanted was not always clear, but it was crystal clear what they did not want: a continuation of the failed "liberal democracy" that was captured by the elites; even in those rare moments when the voice of the people prevailed, the system was too slow, too prone to veto points controlled by elites, and too corrupt to long serve the needs of the people.

With the rise of Donald Trump, the Tea Party found its savior. Trump was a disruptor who verbally attacked the status quo, saw the elite as his as well as the Tea Party's enemy, was the voice for their concerns, and promised to "drain the swamp" (the corrupt and selfish elites). "I love the less educated," he announced at a 2016 campaign rally, and he promised to take back America from "them." The *them* was first and foremost seen in the person of Barack Obama.

Trump had been for years stoking the flames of a conspiracy that alleged Obama was not born in the United States and was, thus, an illegitimate president. Race and white status anxiety were powerful forces in the Tea Party movement, and as America was in the process of change, many white voters felt threatened, and Donald Trump became their outlet.

Trump's four years as president was characterized as a series of challenges to America's liberal democracy. Trump ordered a ban on all Muslims entering the United States, but the courts stopped him. Trump promised to "build a wall" on the U.S. southern border, but Congress refused to fund it. He promised to repeal and replace Obamacare, but he failed to offer a replacement, and Congress did not have the stomach for a fight. Trump wanted to pressure the leader of a foreign country (Ukraine) to find dirt on Joe Biden, his likely 2020 presidential rival, but Congress impeached him for it. At virtually every turn, Trump came into conflict with the checks-and-balances, rule-of-law system and the separation of powers. His bold assertions of plenary authority notwithstanding (e.g., "I have an Article II, where I have the right to do whatever I want as president"), the American system of laws and checks and balances stood in the way of Trump achieving several of his key policy goals.

This infuriated Trump's followers, along with his Tea Party supporters. Like Trump, they saw the swamp as blocking Trump's path and corruptly stealing powers. They wanted to take back America, and Trump was just the man to do it. Rule of law? Slow and corrupt. Donald Trump? Their political savior.

The Tea Party represented the American version of the wave of populist discontent spreading in other industrial nations. Trump did not create this movement, but he harnessed the anger and American discontent and rode that wave to power. His style and charisma seduced his base, and he promised to be their champion. The limitations of a liberal democratic regime? Impediments to be swept away. Populists demanded that when elected, leaders have real power.[30] Proponents of the rule of law had a different idea.

When Trump lost the 2020 election, the president claimed fraud, corruption, and that the election had been stolen. Recount after recount, failed court case after failed court case, could not convince Trump or his base or a majority of the Republican Party that he lost in a free and fair election. Trump pressured several state election officials to change their vote totals, but with no success. The rules, the laws, norms, and procedures when followed scrupulously had Trump losing. But he would not acknowledge or accept the results. Instead, he pressured his vice president, Mike Pence, as presiding officer in the Senate, to *not* accept the electoral votes of the states and help him overturn the election results. Pence refused.

Failing this, Trump organized a Washington, D.C., "Stop the Steal" rally on January 6, 2021, on the morning the electoral votes were to be certified by Congress. At that rally, Trump called on his supporters to "fight" and to march to the Capitol ("I'll be there with you," he said, although he was a no-show). He told his followers:

> You'll never take back our country with weakness. You have to show strength, and you have to be strong.
>
> Something is wrong here, something is really wrong, can't have happened and we fight, we fight like hell, and if you don't fight like hell, you're not going to have a country anymore.
>
> So we are going to—we are going to walk down Pennsylvania Avenue, I love Pennsylvania Avenue, and we are going to the Capitol, and we are going to try and give—the Democrats are hopeless, they are never voting for anything, not even one vote but we are going to try—give our Republicans, the weak ones because the strong ones don't need any of our help, we're try—going to try and give them the kind of pride and boldness that they need to take back our country. So, let's walk down Pennsylvania Avenue.

And walk down Pennsylvania Avenue they did. Trump followers—many believing they were following the president's orders—marched to the Capitol, some shouting "Hang Mike Pence" or "Nancy [Pelosi], we're coming for you," broke in, destroyed property, assaulted law enforcement officials, and people died.

The insurrection against the government of the United States failed to put Trump back in the White House for another term, and it revealed just how fragile our democracy can be. Liberal democracy, based on the rule of law, was challenged by Donald

Trump and his base. But did Trump's illiberal brand of leadership portend the end of liberal government and the emergence of government by strongmen? Can liberal democracy survive an age of globalization and hyperchange? Should it?

Of course, giving so much power to one person raises the question raised by the Roman poet Juvenal: *Quis custodiet ipsos custodes*? ("Who will guard the guardians?") Is it safe (or wise) to confer so much power onto one strongman and trust that said power will be exercised wisely and well? What checks, guarantees, and rights does a citizen have when confronted with the power of a strongman at the helm of government? In 1776, the strong leader was the problem to be solved; in an illiberal democracy, the strong leader is seen as the solution to the problem of government gridlock and inadequacy; but what is to prevent the strong leader from abusing power?

MY VIEW

For all its faults, I'll take liberal democracy. Slow, yes; imperfect, certainly; ideal, no. But as Winston Churchill reminded us, "Many forms of government have been tried, and will be tried in this world of sin and woe. No one pretends that democracy is perfect or all-wise. Indeed it has been said that democracy is the worst form of Government except for all those other forms that have been tried from time to time."[31]

CONCLUSION

To again quote Winston Churchill, "A monarchy is a merchantman which sails well, but will sometimes strike a rock, and go to the bottom; a republic is like a raft which will never sink, but then your feet are always in the water."[32] Autocracies and monarchies may run splendidly when a beneficent leader is at the helm. But what is to guarantee that we get "one of the good ones"? Yes, autocracies may rise to high levels, but they may also "strike a rock." Democracies and republics may be less efficient and messier, and yes, we always seem to get our feet wet, but we so rarely come aground on the shoals. Is this a case of damning liberal democracy with faint praise, or is "muddling along" good enough?

Autocrats get things done. An Augustus of Rome got several good things done; a Caligula made a big mess of just about everything. High highs, and low lows. Democracies only rarely get the big things done well. But they often incrementally move us in the right direction. Is good good-enough?

CONCLUSION

The American presidency has adjusted and adapted during the past two-hundred-plus years. It is a protean office, and this ability to change, be flexible, and adapt guarantees both the office's ongoing relevance and importance in our lives and in the life of the republic.

But our eighteenth-century Constitution is asked to help govern a twenty-first-century superpower. Do old models work or do we need a new model of leadership for a new age? It is sometimes useful to conceptualize something new using metaphors. So, what is the proper metaphor for the transition to this new twenty-first-century leadership that is required? I would suggest that the contrast between the symphony orchestra, with a strong, dominant conductor physically at the helm, represents the "old" model, while the jazz ensemble represents the leadership model for the future. In the jazz ensemble, different members of the group take the lead at different times, and while there is a certain pattern from which they start, the process of arriving at the conclusion depends on the mood, talents, cohesiveness, skill, and vision of all the players. It is more of a group venture than the triumph of the strong central leader. Or another way to look at this transformation is to compare a photograph to a

Jackson Pollock painting. The photograph is literal and clear; the Pollock painting is more abstract, harder to understand, and more complex.

Thus, the key skills for a leader of this new and threatening world are *flexibility* and *adaptability*. There is no "plan B." Leaders must adapt themselves and help their constituencies to adapt. And the only way to do this is for our leaders to be flexible and adaptive themselves.

A useful thought experiment would be to try to imagine the presidency in 2040. Have the guardrails of democracy held strong? Is the separation of powers still a vital element in government? How strong—or weak—is Congress vis-à-vis the presidency? Is the past prelude, that is, is the presidency bigger and stronger, or have we learned to "tame the prince"? Where do we stand regarding the Goldilocks dilemma? Who "declares" war? Is our system more democratic or more autocratic? Are our parties strong and functional? Are citizens connected to the government or are they alienated? Is the presidency "the government" or do we still have a robust three-part government?

Harvard University leadership expert Ron Heifetz has written extensively about the *adapting function* of leaders.[1] If there is a technical solution to a problem, leadership is not necessary, but as Heifetz notes, it is when society or organizations need to adapt, to change, that leadership is needed. Leadership comes into play when we do not have a ready technical solution to a problem and need a strategy to help us adapt. Adaptive challenges are recurrent problems, the solutions to which are outside of our current repertoire; we need to adapt our behavior to deal with this challenge or threat.

Leaders can help us recognize where the old or technical solutions fall short, identify needed alterations, mobilize the public to change, assist this transition, and develop and promote a vision of an alternative future. Adaptive leadership can be risky, yet it is necessary and rewarding. Getting us to face the demands we confront and offering adaptive changes is what leading is all about.[2]

It is hard to imagine an America without the often frustrating, even maddeningly slow checks and balances that *do* slow the power of change and inhibit government action. And while some say that "we should run government like a business," that superficial appeal, while sounding good, would undo the checks and balances built into our system of government.

It is legitimate to pose the question in a different way: Is our system—that worked so well for two-hundred-plus years—no longer a good fit for a global superpower in an age of hyperchange? Would we be wise to streamline and modernize our system a bit? "Things change," and we must accept that the coat that fit us at age thirteen no longer fits. It would be foolish not to get a new coat, one that fits. So too with our government.

Or are the values and aspirations of the framers universal and as applicable now as in their times? Are their enduring values and ideas worth protecting? Does our political system need some minor tinkering or major surgery?

The six questions/debates that form the core of this book ask us to take a deep dive into the meaning and role of the presidency in American government. What was it designed to do? How did it evolve over time? What has it become? And is the presidency of today a good fit for our status as a twenty-first-century superpower?

From the beginning, the framers knew what they did *not* want (a mob or a monarchy to rule) but were less clear about what they did want. A republican executive, yes, but how was this to be operationalized? There were many moving parts; would they all work together?

The presidency was and remains "contested territory." People from different and contrasting approaches, ideologies, and perspectives see different things in this office. Some want a big, powerful presidency to solve big problems. Others want the government, and the presidency, to be less obtrusive. From the start, we've disagreed about this uniquely American institution.

What do these six questions mean for the future of the American presidency? How do the questions inform us as we seek to define the role of the presidency in contemporary politics? And how malleable is the office? Yes, it's sure to grow or shrink depending on the needs of the moment and power sense of the incumbent, but is it so elastic that it has no central core?

The presidency is flexible, adaptable, able to rise and shrink with the nature of the times and the timber of the incumbent. It is also capable of being elevated or degraded depending on the quality of character of each president.

Our answers to these questions matter as our responses will, in a very real way, shape the presidency of tomorrow. Our reactions to presidents and presidential authority send a message to all presidents who follow. Candidates and presidents will usually give in to what we want. This is both the strength and the weakness of democratic-based government.

Perhaps we should both pay respect to the Madisonian system while searching for ways to better adapt it to the twenty-first century. The Goldilocks dilemma is real and inherent in the constitutional ambiguity of the office. Must we leave it at that?

"A Republic, if you can keep it." That was Benjamin Franklin's response when asked as he left the 1787 convention whether the country had been given a democracy or a monarchy. Yes, in the end, it is up to us. We can decide. Our views on politics and the presidency matter. Our views will shape the presidency of the future.

It is an awesome responsibility, one we ought to take very seriously. It demands that we develop informed opinions that are based on evidence. It demands that we be informed, caring, and concerned citizens.

In a commencement address at Cornell University on June 1, 1968, John Gardner, former U.S. secretary of health, education, and welfare (1965–1968), said that we should "Pity the leader caught between unloving critics and uncritical lovers."

He wondered how people in the future would look back on us and believed they might conclude that citizens in our age:

> Were caught in savage crossfire between uncritical lovers and unloving critics. On the one side, those who love their institutions tended to smother them in an embrace of death, loving their rigidities more than their promise, shielding them from life—giving criticism. On the other side, there arose a breed of critics without love, skilled in demolition but untutored in the arts by which human institutions are nurtured and strengthened and made to flourish. Between the two the institutions perished.
>
> The twenty-third-century scholars understood that where human institutions were concerned, love without criticism brings stagnation, and criticism without love brings distraction. And they emphasized that the swifter the pace of change, the more lovingly men had to care for and criticize their institutions to keep them intact through the turbulent passages.
>
> In short, men must be discriminating appraisers of their society, knowing coolly and precisely what it is about the society that thwarts or limits them and therefore needs modification. And so must they be discriminating protectors of their institutions, preserving those features that nourish and strengthen them and make more free. To fit themselves for such tasks, they must be sufficiently serious to study their institutions, sufficiently dedicated to become expert in the art of modifying them.[3]

Two hundred thirty-five years ago, the framers invented a new form of government and a new office: a presidency. We have nearly fifty presidents whose experience, trials, and successes we can draw upon. And I've been teaching and writing about the presidency for more than forty years. You'd think I might have learned something by now. So, what is the added value derived from nearly a half century of studying the presidency; what do I "know" of the presidency? What are the *presidential axioms* that I—and we presidency scholars—truly *know*? What are the "iron laws" of the presidency?

In the broad sweep of presidential history, we've had our highs and lows, our greats, near greats, and ingrates in the White House. What does this 235-year history of the office reveal about what it takes to be a successful president?

Machiavelli insisted that as human nature was the same then as now, we would be wise to derive lessons from leaders of the past. That was the very basis of his advice in *The Prince*. History unlocks the door to the mystery of success.

Of course, as Henry Ford so unartfully put it, history is "just one damn thing after another." Are we dealing merely with one damn president after another? Or is history, as Macbeth so artfully put it, "a tale full of sound and fury signifying nothing?" A series of tall tales and interesting stories but of limited utility? Perhaps Mark Twain was closest to the mark when he noted that "history does not repeat itself, but it does rhyme." And what of George Santayana's admonition: "Those who cannot remember the past are condemned to repeat it"? If the past offers us any guidance, it is in the presidential axioms that follow.

The Presidency Is Necessary and Dangerous

American presidents have helped us reach some of our highest aspirations. Some have helped us to confront prejudice, to preserve the Union during the Civil War; have led us through depressions and world wars; and have called upon the better angels within us.

Other presidents appealed to what was dark within us, to racial hatreds and religious bigotry; supported slavery and waged genocide against Native Americans[4]; attacked immigrants; and encouraged insurgency against our government.

In a dangerous world, presidential leadership might be necessary while adversaries wish us harm. Plus, presidential leadership can help us solve problems and achieve our goals. But the same institution that can help protect us may also be dangerous to democracy.

As George Bernard Shaw so aptly reminds us, "you cannot have power for good without having power for evil too. Even mother's milk nourishes murderers as well as heroes."[5] So, what empowers presidents who do "good" also creates opportunities to do ill. Only with a Congress and court system that lives up to its constitutional responsibility to, among other things, check abuses of power, and an educated and engaged citizenry can we hope to empower presidents to do good and stop presidents who will do harm.

Experience Matters

As a generalization, it is better to have more experience than less. Presidents such as Franklin D. Roosevelt, Joe Biden, and George H. W. Bush had vast experience in governing. They did not have to learn on the job. By contrast, Donald Trump is the only president in history to enter office with zero military and political experience.

Of course, even experienced presidents can blunder. Lyndon B. Johnson in Vietnam or Richard Nixon in Watergate are but two of the most vivid examples. But in any job interview, a potential employer (in this case, us) would want to know what experience a job seeker has that would make that individual qualified for the job at hand. Some executive (mayor or governor), legislative (state legislature or Congress), Washington D.C., and foreign policy experience would be valuable. And yes, Abraham Lincoln and Barack Obama had limited experience, so experience is no guarantee of success, just as limited experience is no guarantee of failure. But for me, if I need my car repaired or brain surgery, I would be inclined to hire a trained, experienced mechanic or brain surgeon (always being careful not to mix up the two).

One Number Tells Most of the Story

The passage of landmark legislation is the measure of a successful presidency.[6] By this measure, the two presidents in the past one hundred years who stand out far and above all others are Franklin D. Roosevelt and Lyndon B. Johnson. Both were seasoned politicians who had the ability to think and act strategically. In FDR's "first hundred days,"[7] he was able to get Congress to pass multiple significant bills that created a "New Deal" for America. LBJ, in the aftermath of the assassination of John F. Kennedy, was able to get Congress to pass a slew of major bills in what was called "The Great Society" program.[8]

What did these two successful presidents have in common? One of the factors they shared, and the most important contribution to their success, was a large majority of their party in control of Congress. This partisan advantage allowed FDR and LBJ to rely on party voting, and even if they lost a few Democratic legislators here or there, they had such a large partisan cushion—in the seventy-third Congress (1933–1935), the Democrats held a 313–117 seat advantage in the House and a 59–36 seat advantage in the Senate; in the eighty-ninth Congress (1965–1967), the Democrats held a 295–140 seat advantage in the House and a 68–32 seat advantage in the Senate—that they could still pass major legislation.

Compare their positions to that of Donald Trump or Joe Biden. Both faced tightly held or split control of Congress, with little or no margin to lose votes. It should not surprise us that FDR and LBJ won so often; nor should we be surprised that Trump and Biden had a difficult time getting Congress to move. While there are a number of factors that contribute to presidential success in Congress, the number one factor is the number of a president's party members in Congress.

The Office Does Not Elevate, It Reveals

Many of us embrace the romantic notion that upon assuming the presidency, the new president, inspired by the awesome power and responsibility of the job, and cognizant that he or she occupies the office once held by Washington, Lincoln, and the two Roosevelts, will somehow be elevated to fit the august stature of the job. But this is not a romance movie, and while it must be inspiring to walk into the Oval Office on day one of a new presidency, and as much as we may wish it, "you are who you are." Men of character were men of character *before* they walked into the presidency. The job shines a spotlight *revealing* who that person is. Lincoln was revealed as Lincoln, Trump as Trump, Nixon as Nixon. You are what you bring to the office.

There May Be a "Design Flaw" in the Constitution

Is there a major design flaw in the Constitution? Spoiler alert: most scholars would say yes. So, what might that design flaw be? Many scholars compare the U.S. separation-of-powers model to the UK's parliamentary or fusion-of-powers model, finding the U.S. model wanting. The separation model is slow, difficult to move, usually ends in delay and deadlock, and often fails to deliver. By contrast, the British fusion of power (joining the executive and the legislature) is geared to decision-making. A majority in Parliament—unlike the U.S. Congress—can and does pass its manifesto (platform) into law. Elections empower governments in the United Kingdom, while in the United States, getting elected merely gives one the opportunity to grab power that is elusive.

While there is no way the United States will become a parliamentary system, there are ways to streamline the U.S. government a bit. All federal officeholders (president, House, Senate) could be simultaneously elected to four-year terms, thereby giving a new president the opportunity to gain a mandate to govern. Fast-track legislation might also be useful, as would guarantees that the Senate must vote—up or down—on a president's nominees. These and other possible reforms are designed to provide less separation and more efficiency. We may not be able to fully convert the framers' design flaw (Madison's "curse," not his "gift" to us), but we clearly need to make the government better able to actually govern.

Additionally, we should consider how to bring a president's *war powers* under greater constitutional control, eliminate the *Electoral College*, and move to *direct popular election* of the president; bring more common sense to the selection process by instituting *regional primaries* and decreasing the role of *money* in our political process; *depoliticize* the law enforcement agencies of the federal government (including the Department of Justice); give the *impeachment* process more teeth as a way of holding presidents to account; give the president a *line-item veto* in the budget; repeal the *Twenty-Second Amendment*; and have a serious *national conversation* about just what we want of our presidents in the twenty-first century.[9]

Accepting the current constitutional contours of the presidency only invites trouble. The office was invented in the eighteenth century. Thus, we must ask: Is the Constitution suited to a twenty-first-century superpower? Do we need to do some major surgery or only tinkering?

Trust Matters

In 1958, when pollsters asked a sampling of the American public if they had confidence in the government to do the right thing almost all the time or most of the time, 73 percent said "Yes." In 1974, when asked that question, 77 percent said "Yes." By the mid 1970s, that number began to take a steady nosedive. The war in Vietnam, Watergate, economic downturns, the Iran-Contra scandal, Bill Clinton's impeachment, Newt Gingrich's slash-and-burn politics, the war in Iraq, and Hurricane Katrina; then, the Trump presidency. All contributed to the steady decline in the public's trust of government.

Trust matters.[10] With America's pronounced trust deficit, we are suspicious of government, untrusting of each other, and the bonds of unity break. Trust lubricates; a lack of trust hardens. And let us remember that our system was designed by the people who held a distrust of government and did not want to make it easy for the government to act. Our political system, hard to move in the best of circumstances, usually breaks down into paralysis and deadlock unless we can find ways to work together. And if we are so distrustful,[11] we cannot move the machinery of government for the public good.

All Our Heroes Have Feet of Clay

Do we expect too much of our presidents? And are we too unforgiving of their shortcomings? Our fascination with movie and comic-book superheroes distorts our expectation level, as do candidates themselves who make bold campaign promises only to let us down once in office.

There is an old saying, "Every four years we pick a president, and for the next four years we make it our mission to pick him apart." Are we too hard, too unforgiving? Probably. No person, and certainly no president, is perfect. Our presidents are human. We should see them as such and expect them to make progress, not achieve perfection.

The ideal president is the *selfless servant*. George H. W. Bush and Barack Obama come to mind. Yes, both were ambitious and striving; wallflowers tend not to seek the presidency. But both men had a clear and strong sense of self. Perfect they were not, but one never got the sense that they had to be president. A lust for power and office led Donald Trump to promote the "big lie" that the 2020 presidential election was a fraud, and he actively attempted to get the election results overturned. Oh, but the damage he did along the way.

Two hundred thirty-five years of presidents, good and bad, great and not so great. And in the end, our experiment with liberal democracy endures. We cannot secure its future without our active support. "A Republic, if you can keep it," is how Benjamin Franklin described this bold experiment. If *we* can keep it.

Republics are fragile entities. They need constant care and feeding. If ignored or left unattended to, they can wither away, fall into the wrong hands, and be transformed into autocracies. The many benefits derived from living in (however imperfect) a constitutional republic require us to do some heavy democratic lifting. Ours is not a machine that will go of itself. It is ours to keep or to lose.

ACKNOWLEDGMENTS

I hereby acknowledge that had it not been for the following people, I would still be sitting at my computer, trying to remember how to do footnotes or how to number pages, and no one would be reading this book: Noura Alavi, graduate assistant; Elsie Mares, Riley McCoy, Juliana Angel, and Tessa Muller, student interns. My deepest thanks to you for all you did to bring this book to life. You are "da best." And when one of you becomes president of the United States, remember: Genovese for ambassador to Italy.

A note on the use of the male pronoun: Throughout this book, I refer to presidents as "he." I do so for two reasons: (1) Of course, all presidents have been men; and (2) consistency and efficiency in reading and writing. This is not meant to exclude women from the conversation, but women have historically been shut out from the political process, and while that is changing, the presidency has been a gender-exclusive office since its inception. May that change very soon.

In fact, in 2016 we had our first real chance to elect a woman, but Hillary Clinton lost in the Electoral College to Donald Trump (she won the popular vote by nearly three million votes). Then, in 2020 Senator Kamala Harris was elected vice president in Joe Biden's successful bid for the presidency. Glass ceilings are being broken, but there is one more that will break, and soon.

NOTES

INTRODUCTION

1. See Edward S. Corwin, "Woodrow Wilson and the Presidency," *Virginia Law Review* 42, no. 6 (1956): 766.
2. Walter Bagehot, *The English Constitution* (Oxford: Oxford University Press, 2001).
3. For an examination of the constitutional presidency, see Louis Fisher, *Constitutional Conflicts Between Congress and the President*, 5th ed. (Lawrence: University Press of Kansas, 2007).
4. *Youngstown Sheet & Tube Co. v. Sawyer*, 343 U.S. 579, 635 (1952) (Jackson, J., concurring).
5. *Myers v. United States*, 272 U.S. 52 (1926) (Brandeis, J., dissenting).
6. John Dickerson, *The Hardest Job in the World: The American Presidency* (New York: Random House, 2020), xxiii.
7. See William G. Howell, *Power Without Persuasion: The Politics of Direct Presidential Action* (Princeton, NJ: Princeton University Press, 2003), xiv.
8. Richard E. Neustadt, *Presidential Power* (New York: Vintage, 1960).
9. See Thomas E. Cronin, Michael A. Genovese, and Meena Bose, *The Paradoxes of the American Presidency*, 6th ed. (Oxford: Oxford University Press, 2022).
10. See Maria Konnikova, *Mastermind: How to Think Like Sherlock Holmes* (London: Penguin, 2013).
11. Sir Arthur Conan Doyle, *The Sign of the Four* (1890; repr. Orinda, CA: Sea Wolf Press, 2019), 101.

12. Peter Drucker, *The Effective Executive* (New York: Harper Collins, 1966), 79.

13. See Michael A. Genovese, *The Presidential Dilemma: Leadership in the American System* (New York: Harper Collins, 1995), chap. 2.

1. WHAT IS MORE IMPORTANT, POWER OR PERSUASION?

1. Robert A. Caro, *The Power Broker: Robert Moses and the Fall of New York* (New York: Vintage, 1975).

2. Anthony King, "Foundations of Power," in *Researching the Presidency: Vital Questions, New Approaches*, ed. George C. Edwards III, John H. Kessel, and Bert Rockman (Pittsburgh, PA: University of Pittsburgh Press, 1993), 415–451.

3. Richard E. Neustadt, *Presidential Power* (New York: Vintage, 1960).

4. Kenneth R. Mayer, *With the Stroke of a Pen: Executive Order and Presidential Power* (Princeton, NJ: Princeton University Press, 2001); Phillip J. Cooper, *By Order of the President: The Use and Abuse of Executive Direct Action* (Lawrence: University Press of Kansas, 2002); and Greg Robinson, *By Order of the President* (Cambridge, MA: Harvard University Press, 2001).

5. Charles M. Cameron, *Veto Bargaining: Presidents and the Politics of Negative Power* (Cambridge: Cambridge University Press, 2000); and Patricia Heidotting Conley, *Presidential Mandates: How Elections Shape the National Agenda* (Chicago: University of Chicago Press, 2001).

6. William G. Howell, *Power Without Persuasion: The Politics of Direct Presidential Action* (Princeton, NJ: Princeton University Press, 2003), 14–15.

7. See Thomas E. Cronin, Michael A. Genovese, and Meena Bose, *The Paradoxes of the American Presidency*, 6th ed. (Oxford: Oxford University Press, 2022).

8. See Jon R. Bond and Richard Fleisher, *The President in the Legislative Arena* (Chicago: University of Chicago Press, 1992); Brandice Canes-Wrone, *Who Leads Whom? President, Policy, and the Public* (Chicago: University of Chicago Press, 2005); and George C. Edwards III, *The Strategic President Persuasion and Opportunity in Presidential Leadership* (Princeton, NJ: Princeton University Press, 2009).

9. Canes-Wrone, *Who Leads Whom?*

10. Anne C. Pluta, "Reassessing the Assumptions Behind the Evolution of Popular Presidential Communication," *Presidential Studies Quarterly* 45, no. 1 (March 2015).

11. Julia Azari, *Delivering the President's Message: The Changing Politics of the Presidential Mandate* (Ithaca, NY: Cornell University Press, 2014).

12. Hans A. von Spakovsky, "DACA Is Unconstitutional, as Obama Admitted," Heritage Foundation, September 8, 2017.

13. Interview, "Michael McConnell on Executive Orders, DACA, and the Constitution," Stanford Law School, September 6, 2017.

14. Joseph S. Nye Jr., "Propaganda Isn't the Way," *International Herald Tribune*, January 10, 2003.

15. Joseph S. Nye Jr., *Bound to Lead: The Changing Nature of American Power* (New York: Basic Books, 1990).

2. WHAT MATTERS MORE, THE INDIVIDUAL OR THE INSTITUTION?

1. See this approach applied with grave consequences in Andy Slavitt, *Preventable* (New York: St. Martin's Press, 2021).

2. Thomas Carlyle, *On Heroes, Hero-Worship, and the Heroic in History* (London: James Fraser, 1841), 47.

3. Herbert Spencer, *The Study of Sociology* (London: Henry S. King & Co., 1873), 33.

4. For a brief examination of Napoleon as a dominating leader, see Andrew Roberts, *Leadership in War: Essential Lessons from Those Who Made History* (London: Penguin, 2019), chap. 1.

5. Nico Mouton, "A Literary Perspective on the Limits of Leadership: Tolstoy's Critique of the Great Man Theory," *Leadership* 15, no. 1 (December 11, 2017): 99.

6. Archie Brown, "Does Leadership Matter?" *Prospect Magazine*, February 18, 2016.

7. John Dickerson, *The Hardest Job in the World: The American Presidency* (New York: Random House, 2020), 70.

8. See Kendrick A. Clements, "Woodrow Wilson and Administrative Reform," *Presidential Studies Quarterly* 28, no. 2 (1998): 325.

9. David E. Lewis and Mark D. Richardson, "The Very Best People: Donald Trump and the Management of Executive Personnel," *Presidential Studies Quarterly* 1, no. 1 (January 2021): 51–70; and Karen M. Hult, "Assessing the Trump White House," *Presidential Studies Quarterly* 1, no. 1 (January 2021): 35–50.

10. Dickerson, *Hardest Job in the World*, xxix.

11. Chris Whipple, *The Gatekeepers: How the White House Chiefs of Staff Define Every Presidency* (New York: Crown, 2017).

12. Quotes in Theodore Sorensen, *Decision-Making in the White House: The Olive Branch or the Arrows* (New York: Columbia University Press, 2005), xxix.

13. Barbara W. Tuchman, *The March of Folly: From Troy to Vietnam* (New York: Ballantine, 1984).

14. George E. Reedy, *The Twilight of the Presidency* (Calcutta: Signet, 1971).

15. Tuchman, *March of Folly*, 7.

16. Tuchman, *March of Folly*, 381.

17. Michael Lewis, *The Fifth Risk* (New York: Norton, 2019).

18. Kenneth R. Mayer, "The Random Walk Presidency," *Presidential Studies Quarterly* 1, no. 1 (January 2021): 71–95.

19. Michael Lewis, *The Premonition: A Pandemic Story* (New York: Norton, 2021).

20. Jeff Tollefson, "How Trump Damaged Science—And Why It Could Take Decades to Recover," *Nature* 586 (October 5, 2020): 190–94.

21. Libby Cathey, "With String of Attacks on Doctors and Experts, Trump Takes Aim at Science: Analysis," *ABC News*, August 6, 2020.

22. Bob Woodward, *Rage* (New York: Simon & Schuster, 2020), 391–92.

23. German Lopez, "How Trump Let Covid-19 Win," *Vox*, September 22, 2020, https://www.vox.com/future-perfect/21366624/trump-covid -coronavirus-pandemic-failure.

24. Jake Tapper, "That's a Confession," *State of the Union*, CNN, March 29, 2021.

25. Michael A. Genovese, "The Rise of the Anti-Analytical Presidency," *History News Network*, October 4, 2020.

26. Walter Williams, *Mismanaging America: The Rise of the Anti-Analytic Presidency* (Lawrence: University Press of Kansas, 1990).

3. DID THE FRAMERS INVENT A POWERFUL UNITARY EXECUTIVE OR A LIMITED CONSTITUTIONAL OFFICE?

1. See Graham G. Dodds, *The Unitary Presidency* (Abingdon, UK: Routledge, 2020); and Jeffrey Crouch, Mark J. Rozell, and Mitchel A. Sollenberger, *The Unitary Executive Theory: A Danger to Constitutional Government* (Lawrence: University Press of Kansas, 2020).

2. Michael A. Genovese, "Power Above Principle: How Conservatives Came to Embrace Presidential Power," *Ohio Northern University Law Review* 47, no. 1 (2021): 117–64.

3. Ray Raphael, *Mr. President, How and Why the Founders Created a Chief Executive* (New York: Vintage, 2012); and Thomas E. Ricks, *First Principles: What America's Founders Learned from the Greeks and Romans and How That Shaped Our Country* (New York: Harper, 2020).

4. Bill Clinton, "Let's Make a Deal," C-SPAN, Presidential Leadership Scholars Program, September 12, 2014.

5. See Genovese, "Power Above Principle."

6. Crouch, Rozell, and Sollenberger, *Unitary Executive Theory*, 2.

7. Crouch, Rozell, and Sollenberger, *Unitary Executive Theory*, 2.

8. Crouch, Rozell, and Sollenberger, *Unitary Executive Theory*, 2.

9. Genovese, "Power Above Principle."

10. Steven G. Calabresi and Christopher S. Yoo, *The Unitary Executive: Presidential Power from Washington to Bush* (New Haven, CT: Yale University Press, 2008), 4.

11. Daniel P. Franklin, *Extraordinary Measures: The Exercise of Prerogative Powers in the United States* (Pittsburgh, PA: University of Pittsburgh Press, 1991).

12. Genovese, "Power Above Principle."

13. President George W. Bush addresses a Joint Congress About the War on Terror, AP Archive, July 31, 2015, https://www.youtube.com/watch?v=TYnx-c8pF34.

14. The Authorization for the Use of Military Force (ALMF) (2001), https://www.govinfo.gov/content/pkg/PLAW-107publ40/pdf/PLAW-107publ40.pdf.

15. See Michael Haas, *George W. Bush: War Animal?* (Westport, CT: Praeger, 2008).

16. See Crouch, Rozell, and Sollenberger, *Unitary Executive Theory*, 2–5.

17. Eric A. Posner and Adrian Vermuele, *The Executive Unbound: After the Madisonian Republic* (Oxford: Oxford University Press, 2013).

4. WHICH IS MORE VALUABLE, CHARACTER OR COMPETENCE?

1. For a more comprehensive treatment of the paradoxical nature of the president, see Thomas E. Cronin, Michael A. Genovese, and Meena Bose, *The Paradoxes of the American Presidency*, 6th ed. (Oxford: Oxford University Press, 2021).

2. David H. Souter, Harvard commencement remarks, May 27, 2010, http://news.harvard.edu/gazette/story/2010/05/text-of-justice-david-souters-speech/.

3. George E. Reedy, *The Twilight of the Presidency: From Johnson to Reagan*, rev. ed. (New York: Dutton, 1987), 42.

4. See Stanley Fish, "Integrity or Craft: The Leadership Question," *Opinionator* (blog), *New York Times*, December 9, 2007, https://opinionator.blogs.nytimes.com/2007/12/09/integrity-or-craft-the-leadership-question/.

5. Doris Kearns Goodwin: "Six Essential Traits a President Needs," *History*, October 24, 2018; "What Makes a Good President?" [press release], American Psychological Association, August 1, 2000, https://www.apa.org/news/press/releases/2000/08/presidents; and Deseri Garcia, "9 Things Great Presidents and Leaders Have in Common," *Vida Adventura*, August 14, 2019.

6. Dennis F. Thompson, "Constitutional Character: Virtues and Vices in Presidential Leadership," *Presidential Studies Quarterly* 40, no. 1 (March 2010): 24.

7. George E. Reedy, *The Twilight of the Presidency* (Calcutta: Signet, 1971), 41.

8. Jonathan Alter, *His Very Best: Jimmy Carter, a Life* (New York: Simon & Schuster, 2020).

9. James Cannon, *Gerald R. Ford: An Honorable Life* (Ann Arbor: University of Michigan Press, 2013).

10. John F. Harris, *The Survivor: Bill Clinton in the White House* (New York: Random House, 2006).

11. Michael A. Genovese, *The Nixon Presidency: Power and Politics in Turbulent Times* (Westport, CT: Greenwood Press, 1990).

12. Michael D'Antonio, *The Hunting of Hillary: The Forty-Year Campaign to Destroy Hillary Clinton* (New York: Thomas Dunne Books, 2020).

13. Jonathan Karl, *Front Row at the Trump Show* (New York: Dutton, 2020).

14. Karl, *Front Row at the Trump Show*.

15. "Bread and circuses" (*panem et circenses*), from Roman poet Juvenal (born around 55 CE), is meant to describe how some leaders pander to the public by winning approval not by excellence in governing but by offering the public candy and entertainment thus satisfying basic hungers.

16. T. S. Eliot, *The Cocktail Party* (Boston: Mariner Books, 1964).

17. Lara Brown, *Amateur Hour: Presidential Character and the Question of Leadership* (Abingdon, UK: Routledge, 2020).

18. Baltasar Gracián, *The Art of Worldly Wisdom* (Boulder, CO: Shambhala, 1993), 67.

19. Michael Gerson, "Ron Johnson Isn't a Republican Outlier," *Washington Post*, March 22, 2021, https://www.washingtonpost.com/opinions/ron-johnson-isnt-a-republican-outlier/2021/03/22/fde3d8da-8b3d-11eb-a730-1b4ed9656258_story.html.

5. WHAT IS MORE IMPORTANT, SKILL OR OPPORTUNITY?

1. See Michael A. Genovese, Todd L. Belt, and William W. Lammers, *The Presidency and Domestic Policy: Comparing Leadership Styles, FDR to Biden*, 4th ed. (Abingdon, UK: Routledge, 2022).

2. Arthur M. Schlesinger Jr., *The Imperial Presidency* (Boston: Houghton Mifflin, 2004).

3. Michael A. Genovese, *The Presidential Dilemma*, 3rd ed. (Piscataway, NJ: Transaction, 2011), 91.

4. Quoted in Fred I. Greenstein, *The Presidential Difference: Leadership Style from FDR to Clinton* (Princeton, NJ: Princeton University Press, 2001), 17–18.

5. Both of James M. Burns's volumes on FDR, *The Lion and the Fox (1882–1940)* (New York: Open Road Media, 2012) and *Roosevelt: The Soldier of*

Freedom (1940–1945) (New York: Open Road Media, 2012), are worth reading, and rereading.

6. Aaron Wildavsky, "The Two Presidencies," *Trans-Action/Society* 4 (1996): 7.

7. Elizabeth D. Samet, *Leadership* (New York: Norton, 2017), xxvii.

8. Valerie Bunce, *Do New Leaders Make a Difference? Executive Succession and Public Policy Under Capitalism and Socialism* (Princeton, NJ: Princeton University Press, 1981).

9. Daniel Paul Franklin and Michael P. Fix, "The Best of Times and the Worst of Times: Polarization and Presidential Success in Congress," *Congress & the Presidency* 43 (2016): 377–94.

10. See Genovese, Belt, and Lammers, *The Presidency and Domestic Policy.*

11. Quoted in Hedrick Smith, *The Power Game: How Washington Works* (New York: Ballantine, 1988), 331.

12. Bunce, *Do New Leaders Make a Difference?*

13. James P. Pfiffner, "The Carter-Reagan Transition: Hitting the Ground Running," *Presidential Studies Quarterly* 13, no. 4 (Fall 1983): 623–45.

14. For a fuller exploration of the skill/opportunity connection, see Genovese, Belt, and Lammers, *The Presidency and Domestic Policy.*

6. WILL THE FUTURE OF THE U.S. PRESIDENCY BE ONE OF LIBERAL DEMOCRACY OR ILLIBERAL DEMOCRACY?

1. Edmund S. Morgan, *Inventing the People: The Rise of Popular Sovereignty in England and America* (New York: Norton, 1988).

2. Francis Fukuyama, *The End of History and the Last Man* (New York: Free Press, 1992).

3. Fareed Zakaria, "On the Rise of Illiberal Democracy," *Foreign Affairs*, November/ December 1997.

4. "A Tsar Is Born," *The Economist*, October 28, 2017.

5. For a primer on the rise and meaning of populism, see Roger Eatwell and Matthew Goodwin, *National Populism: The Revolt Against Liberal Democracy* (New Orleans: Pelican, 2018).

6. For an examination of the contemporary rise of authoritarian populism, see Pippa Norris and Ronald Inglehart, *Cultural Backlash: Trump,*

Brexit, and Authoritarian Populism (Cambridge: Cambridge University Press, 2019).

7. Bethany Albertson and Shana Gadarian, *Anxious Politics: Citizenship in a Threatening World* (Cambridge: Cambridge University Press, 2015).

8. Monty G. Marshall and Ted Robert Gurr, *Polity IV Project: Political Regime Characteristics and Transitions, 1800–2016* (Vienna, VA: Center for Systemic Peace, 2017), 14.

9. Marshall and Gurr, *Polity IV Project*, 15.

10. See Thomas B. Edsall, "Trump's Tool Kit Does Not Include the Constitution," *New York Times*, February 8, 2018; Edsall's essay discusses evidence from Bright Live Watch's survey on faith in democratic principles.

11. See Cas Mudde and Cristobal Rovira Kaltwasser, *Populism: A Very Short Introduction* (Oxford: Oxford University Press, 2017); and John B. Judis, *The Populist Explosion: How the Great Recession Transformed America and European Politics* (New York: Columbia Global Reports, 2016).

12. Timothy Snyder, *The Road to Unfreedom* (New York: Tim Duggan Books, 2019).

13. See Fukuyama, *End of History*.

14. See Larry M. Bartels, *Unequal Democracy* (Princeton, NJ: Princeton University Press, 2016).

15. Jason Brennan, *Against Democracy* (Princeton, NJ: Princeton University Press, 2017).

16. Yascha Mounk, "America Is Not a Democracy," *The Atlantic*, March 2018.

17. "Globally, Broad Support for Representative and Direct Democracy," Pew Research Center, October 16, 2017, https://www.pewresearch.org/global/wp-content/uploads/sites/2/2017/10/Pew-Research-Center_Democracy-Report_2017.10.16.pdf.

18. Donald F. Kettl, *Can Our Governments Earn Our Trust?* (Cambridge: Polity, 2017).

19. Yascha Mounk and Roberto Stefan Foa, "Yes, People Are Really Turning Away from Democracy," *Wonkblog* (blog), *Washington Post*, December 8, 2016.

20. Tom Ginsburg and Aziz Z. Huq, *How to Save a Constitutional Democracy* (Chicago: University of Chicago Press, 2018).

21. Yascha Mounk, *The People vs. Democracy: Why Our Freedom Is in Danger and How to Save It* (Cambridge, MA: Harvard University Press, 2018).

22. See Mounk, *The People vs. Democracy*, chap. 1.

23. Bagehot, "Long Live the Tory Revolution," *The Economist*, August 3, 2019, 49.

24. Bagehot, "Long Live the Tory Revolution," 49.

25. "Coalitions of Chaos," *The Economist*, August 3, 2019, 50.

26. The brand attractiveness of the word *democracy* is still strong, as reflected in Putin's need to wrap himself in the cloak of democratic legitimacy reveals.

27. R. R. Palmer, *The Age of Democratic Revolution* (Princeton, NJ: Princeton University Press, 2014), xvi.

28. Stephen Levitsky and Daniel Ziblatt, *How Democracies Die* (New York: Crown, 2019).

29. Michael A. Genovese and Todd L. Belt, *The Post-Heroic Presidency* (Westport, CT: Praeger, 2016).

30. See Ruth Ben-Ghiat, *Stronger: Mussolini to the Present* (New York: Norton, 2020); Levitsky and Ziblatt, *How Democracies Die*; Anne Applebaum, *Twilight of Democracy: The Seductive Lure of Authoritarianism* (New York: Doubleday, 2020); William G. Howell and Terry M. Moe, *Presidents, Populism, and the Crisis of Democracy* (Chicago: University of Chicago Press, 2020); and Norris and Inglehardt, *Cultural Backlash*.

31. Winston Churchill, *Churchill by Himself: The Definitive Collection of Quotations*, ed. Richard Langworth (New York: Public Affairs, 2008), 574.

32. The quote is first attributed to Fisher Ames; for the Churchill version, see themail@dcwatch, March 21, 2001.

CONCLUSION

1. Ronald A. Heifetz, *Leadership Without Easy Answers* (Cambridge, MA: Harvard University Press, 1998).

2. Thomas E. Cronin and Michael A. Genovese, *Leadership Matters* (Boulder, CO: Paradigm, 2012).

3. John W. Gardner, "Uncritical Lovers, Unloving Critics," *Journal of Educational Research* 62, no. 9 (May–June 1969): 396–99.

4. Michael A. Genovese and Alysa Landry, *U.S. Presidents and the Destruction of Native American Nations* (London: Palgrave Macmillan, 2022).

5. George Bernard Shaw, *Major Barbara* (London: Penguin Classics, 2001).

6. See Michael A. Genovese, Todd L. Belt, and William W. Lammers, *The Presidency and Domestic Policy: Comparing Leadership Styles, FDR to Biden*, 4th ed. (Abingdon, UK: Routledge, 2022).

7. Jonathan Alter, *The Defining Moment: FDR's Hundred Days and the Triumph of Hope* (New York: Simon & Schuster, 2006).

8. Joshua Zeitz, *Building the Great Society: Inside Lyndon Johnson's White House* (New York: Viking, 2018).

9. For a comprehensive reform agenda, see Bob Bauer and Jack Goldsmith, *After Trump: Reconstructing the Presidency* (Washington, DC: Lawfare Institute, 2020).

10. Amy Fried and Douglas B. Harris, *At War with Government* (New York: Columbia University Press, 2021).

11. A little healthy skepticism is a good and necessary thing in a democracy, but we have descended into a deep cynicism that poisons our politics.

SELECTED BIBLIOGRAPHY

Alter, Jonathan. *His Very Best: Jimmy Carter, a Life*. New York: Simon & Schuster, 2020.

Applebaum, Anne. *Twilight of Democracy: The Seductive Lure of Authoritarianism*. New York: Doubleday, 2020.

Bartels, Larry M. *Unequal Democracy*. Princeton, NJ: Princeton University Press, 2016.

Ben-Ghiat, Ruth. *Stronger: Mussolini to the Present*. New York: Norton, 2020.

Brennan, Jason. *Against Democracy*. Princeton, NJ: Princeton University Press, 2017.

Bunce, Valerie. *Do New Leaders Make a Difference? Executive Succession and Public Policy Under Capitalism and Socialism*. Princeton, NJ: Princeton University Press, 1981.

Burns, James M. *The Lion and the Fox (1882–1940)*. New York: Open Road Media, 2012.

——. *Roosevelt: The Soldier of Freedom (1940–1945)*. New York: Open Road Media, 2012.

Calabresi, Steven G., and Christopher S. Yoo. *The Unitary Executive: Presidential Power from Washington to Bush*. New Haven, CT: Yale University Press, 2008.

Cameron, Charles M. *Veto Bargaining: Presidents and the Politics of Negative Power*. Cambridge: Cambridge University Press, 2000.

Cannon, James. *Gerald R. Ford: An Honorable Life*. Ann Arbor: University of Michigan Press, 2013.

Carlyle, Thomas. *On Heroes, Hero-Worship, and the Heroic in History*. London: James Fraser, 1841.

Caro, Robert A. *The Power Broker: Robert Moses and the Fall of New York*. New York: Vintage, 1975.

Churchill, Winston. *Churchill by Himself: The Definitive Collection of Quotations*. Ed. Richard Langworth. New York: Public Affairs, 2008.

Conley, Patricia Heidotting. *Presidential Mandates: How Elections Shape the National Agenda*. Chicago: University of Chicago Press, 2001.

Cooper, Phillip J. *By Order of the President: The Use and Abuse of Executive Direct Action*. Lawrence: University Press of Kansas, 2002.

Cronin, Thomas E., and Michael A. Genovese. *Leadership Matters*. Boulder, CO: Paradigm, 2012.

Cronin, Thomas E., Michael A. Genovese, and Meena Bose. *The Paradoxes of the American Presidency*. 6th ed. Oxford: Oxford University Press, 2022.

Crouch, Jeffrey, Mark J. Rozell, and Mitchel A. Sollenberger. *The Unitary Executive Theory: A Danger to Constitutional Government*. Lawrence: University Press of Kansas, 2020.

D'Antonio, Michael. *The Hunting of Hillary: The Forty-Year Campaign to Destroy Hillary Clinton*. New York: Thomas Dunne Books, 2020.

Dickerson, John. *The Hardest Job in the World: The American Presidency*. New York: Random House, 2020.

Dodds, Graham G. *The Unitary Presidency*. Abingdon, UK: Routledge, 2020.

Doyle, Arthur Conan. *The Sign of the Four*. Orinda, CA: Sea Wolf Press, 2019 (originally published 1890).

Drucker, Peter. *The Effective Executive*. New York: Harper Collins, 1966.

Eatwell, Roger, and Matthew Goodwin. *National Populism: The Revolt Against Liberal Democracy*. New Orleans: Pelican, 2018.

Eliot, T. S. *The Cocktail Party*. Boston: Mariner Books, 1964.

Fisher, Louis. *Constitutional Conflicts Between Congress and the President*. 5th ed. Lawrence: University Press of Kansas, 2007.

Franklin, Daniel P. *Extraordinary Measures: The Exerciser of Prerogative Powers in the United States*. Pittsburgh, PA: University of Pittsburgh Press, 1991.

Fukuyama, Francis. *The End of History and the Last Man*. New York: Free Press, 1992.

Genovese, Michael A. *The Nixon Presidency: Power and Politics in Turbulent Times*. Westport, CT: Greenwood Press, 1990.

——. *The Presidential Dilemma*. 3rd ed. Piscataway, NJ: Transaction, 2011.

——. *The Presidential Dilemma: Leadership in the American System*. New York: Harper Collins, 1995.

Genovese, Michael A., Todd L. Belt, and William W. Lammers. *The Presidency and Domestic Policy: Comparing Leadership Styles, FDR to Biden*. 4th ed. Abingdon, UK: Routledge, 2022.

Ginsburg, Tom, and Aziz Z. Huq. *How to Save a Constitutional Democracy*. Chicago: University of Chicago Press, 2018.

Gracián, Baltasar. *The Art of Worldly Wisdom*. Boulder, CO: Shambhala, 1993.

Greenstein, Fred I. *The Presidential Difference: Leadership Style from FDR to Clinton*. Princeton, NJ: Princeton University Press, 2001.

Haas, Michael. *George W. Bush: War Animal?* Westport, CT: Praeger, 2008.

Harris, John F. *The Survivor: Bill Clinton in the White House*. New York: Random House, 2006.

Heifetz, Ronald A. *Leadership Without Easy Answers*. Cambridge, MA: Harvard University Press, 1998.

Howell, William G. *Power Without Persuasion: The Politics of Direct Presidential Action*. Princeton, NJ: Princeton University Press, 2003.

Howell, William G., and Terry M. Moe. *Presidents, Populism, and the Crisis of Democracy*. Chicago: University of Chicago Press, 2020.

Judis, John B. *The Populist Explosion: How the Great Recession Transformed America and European Politics*. New York: Columbia Global Reports, 2016.

Karl, Jonathan. *Front Row at the Trump Show*. New York: Dutton, 2020.

Kettl, Donald F. *Can Our Governments Earn Our Trust?* Cambridge: Polity, 2017.

Konnikova, Maria. *Mastermind: How to Think Like Sherlock Holmes*. London: Penguin, 2013.

Levitsky, Stephen, and Daniel Ziblatt. *How Democracies Die*. New York: Crown, 2019.

Lewis, Michael. *The Fifth Risk*. New York: Norton, 2019.

——. *The Premonition: A Pandemic Story*. New York: Norton, 2021.

Marshall, Monty G., and Ted Robert Gurr. *Polity IV Project: Political Regime Characteristics and Transitions, 1800–2016*, Vienna, VA: Center for Systemic Peace, 2017.

Mayer, Kenneth. *With the Stroke of a Pen: Executive Order and Presidential Power*. Princeton, NJ: Princeton University Press, 2001.

Morgan, Edmund S. *Inventing the People: The Rise of Popular Sovereignty in England and America*. New York: Norton, 1988.

Mounk, Yascha. *The People vs. Democracy: Why Our Freedom Is in Danger and How to Save It*. Cambridge, MA: Harvard University Press, 2018.

Mudde, Cas, and Cristobal Rovira Kaltwasser. *Populism: A Very Short Introduction*. Oxford: Oxford University Press, 2017.

Neustadt, Richard E. *Presidential Power*. New York: Vintage, 1960.

——. *Presidential Power and the Modern Presidents*. New York: Free Press, 1991.

Norris, Pippa, and Ronald Inglehart. *Cultural Backlash: Trump, Brexit, and Authoritarian Populism*. Cambridge: Cambridge University Press, 2019.

Palmer, R. R. *The Age of Democratic Revolution*. Princeton, NJ: Princeton University Press, 2014.

Posner, Eric A., and Adrian Vermeule. *The Executive Unbound: After the Madisonian Republic*. Oxford: Oxford University Press, 2013.

Raphael, Ray. *Mr. President, How and Why the Founders Created a Chief Executive*. New York: Vintage, 2012.

Reedy, George E. *The Twilight of the Presidency*. Calcutta: Signet, 1971.

——. *The Twilight of the Presidency: From Johnson to Reagan*. Rev. ed. New York: Dutton, 1987.

Ricks, Thomas E. *First Principles: What America's Founders Learned from the Greeks and Romans and How That Shaped Our Country*. New York: Harper, 2020.

Robinson, Greg. *By Order of the President*. Cambridge, MA: Harvard University Press, 2001.

Samet, Elizabeth D. *Leadership*. New York: Norton, 2017.

Schlesinger, Arthur M., Jr. *The Imperial Presidency*. Boston: Houghton Mifflin, 2004.

Smith, Hedrick. *The Power Game: How Washington Works*. New York: Ballantine, 1988.

Snyder, Timothy. *The Road to Unfreedom*. New York: Tim Duggan Books, 2019.

Sorensen, Theodore. *Decision-Making in the White House: The Olive Branch or the Arrows*. New York: Columbia University Press, 2005.

Spencer, Herbert. *The Study of Sociology*. London: Henry S. King & Co., 1873.

Tuchman, Barbara W. *The March of Folly: From Troy to Vietnam*. New York: Ballantine, 1984.

Whipple, Chris. *The Gatekeepers: How the White House Chiefs of Staff Define Every Presidency*. New York: Crown, 2017.

Williams, Walter. *Mismanaging America: The Rise of the Anti-Analytic Presidency*. Lawrence: University Press of Kansas, 1990.

Woodward, Bob. *Rage*. New York: Simon & Schuster, 2020.

INDEX

ACA. *See* Affordable Care Act;
    Obamacare Health Care Act
Acton, Lord, 73
Adams, Abigail, 89
Adams, John Quincy, 89
Affordable Care Act, 23, 39. *See also*
    Obamacare
Afghanistan, 62, 63
Agincourt, 33
Anthony, Mark, 89
anti-analytical presidency, 45, 144
anti-Muslim, 115
anti-terrorism, 63
Argentina, 107, 108
Aristotle, 32, 78
Arkansas, 87
Article I (U.S. Constitution), 3, 4,
    47, 51, 64
Article II (U.S. Constitution), 4, 47,
    51, 59, 62, 64, 122
Articles of Confederation, 4
Athenian democracy, 98
attorney general, U.S., 36

Australia, 107, 108
Austria, 103

Bay of Pigs, 35
Babis, Andrej, 103
Bible, 32
Biden, Joe, 23, 24, 42, 46, 75, 87, 92,
    93, 110, 122, 133, 135, 139
Biden Relief Package, 92
Birx, Dr. Deborah, 41, 43
Bonaparte, Napoleon, 32, 33
Bose, Meena, 10, 34
Brandeis, Louis, 6
Brazil, 107, 108
Brownlow Report, 35
Burke, Edmund, 112
Bush, George H. W., 33, 87, 96, 110,
    117, 133, 138
Bush, George W., 25, 46, 48, 59, 60,
    62, 63, 64, 77, 79, 87, 89, 96, 110

Cabinet, 20, 38
Caesar, Julius, 32, 98

Cameron, Charles, 21

Cameron, David, 115

Canada, 107, 108

Carlyle, Thomas, 32, 34

Caro, Robert, 20

Carter, Jimmy, 13, 70, 71, 74, 75, 76, 87, 96, 110

CDC. *See* Centers for Disease Control and Prevention, U.S.

Chávez, Hugo, 103

checks and balances, 1, 5, 6, 23, 48, 52, 53, 54, 55, 57, 62, 65, 67, 73, 83, 93, 100, 104, 111, 116, 118, 122, 129

chief of staff, 16, 35, 36

Chile, 107, 108

China, 44, 100, 104

Churchill, Winston, 3, 124

Cicero, 89

civil rights, 33, 80

civil service, 20, 21

Civil War, U.S., 55, 57, 60, 61, 97, 132

Clean Waters Restoration Act (1966), 95

Clinton, Bill, 53, 74, 77, 87, 96, 137, 145, 146

Clinton, Hillary, 30, 74, 139

Cold War, 33, 49, 99

Colombia, 107, 108

communism, 49

Conley, Patricia, 21

Constitution, U.S., 2, 3, 4, 5, 6, 8, 11, 15, 19, 20, 47, 49, 50, 51, 52, 53, 54, 55, 56, 57, 58, 59, 60, 61, 62, 63, 64, 65, 67, 72, 73, 83, 98, 100, 127, 130, 133, 135, 136, 137, 138

constitutional republic, 19, 138

Centers for Disease Control and Prevention, U.S. (CDC), 41

Cooper, Philip, 21

Cornell University, 131

Covid Stimulus Package, 23

COVID-19 pandemic, 36, 40, 41, 43, 93

Cox, Archibald, 36

Cox, James M., 87

criminal justice, 109

Cronin, Thomas, 10, 34

Deferred Action for Childhood Arrivals (DACA, 2012), 25, 26

Demonstration Cities Act (1965), 95

Denmark, 115

Department of Housing and Urban Development, U.S., 95

Department of Justice, U.S., 62, 136

Department of Transportation, U.S., 95

Dickerson, John, 35

direct democracy, 105, 106

divine right of kings, 11, 98

divine right of the people, 98

doctrine of necessity, 57, 59, 60, 62

domestic policy, 14, 17, 82, 88, 89

Doyle, Sir Arthur Conan, 12

DREAM Act, 25

Drucker, Pete, 12

Duterte, Rodrigo, 103

economic policy, 17

economic recession, 40, 93

Economist, The, 113, 114

87th Congress, 95

88th Congress, 95

89th Congress, 95, 134
elections, 20, 91, 100, 102, 103, 111,
  115, 136
Eliot, T. S., 76
Electoral College, 136, 139
Emanuel, Rahm, 16
enhanced interrogation, 63
Enlightenment, 98
Erdoğan, Recep Tayyip, 103
Europe, 32, 115, 117
executive action, 20, 26, 62
executive orders, 21, 22, 24, 92

Fair Packaging and Labeling Act
  (1966), 95
Farage, Nigel, 103
Fauci, Dr. Anthony, 41, 43
FDR. *See* Roosevelt, Franklin D.
Federalist Papers, 7, 23, 52, 56, 58, 59
Food and Drug Administration,
  U.S. (FDA), 41
Ford, Gerald, 70, 71, 74, 75, 76, 96, 110
Ford, Henry, 132
foreign affairs, 13, 18, 49, 88, 89, 120
foreign policy, 14, 16, 17, 61, 82, 88, 89,
  94, 120, 122, 134
founders, U.S. 23, 24, 53
France, 101, 103, 107, 108, 115
Franklin, Benjamin, 5, 130
Fukuyama, Francis, 117

Gardner, John, 131
George III (British king), 51
Georgia, 87
Germany, 103, 107, 108
Gerson, Michael, 79
Ghana, 107, 108

Goldilocks dilemma, 17, 23, 81, 82,
  118, 128, 130
Gracian, Balthazar, 78
Great Depression, 32, 55, 60, 61
Great Man Theory, 33, 34, 113
Great Society program (1965–1966),
  134
Greece, 107, 108
Gulf War, 33, 36

Hamdi v. Rumsfeld (2004), 59
Hamilton, Alexander, 5, 7, 23, 52, 53,
  56, 57, 58, 59, 62
hard power, 27
Harding, Warren G., 71
Harvard University, 27, 72, 128
Heifetz, Ron, 128
Higher Education Act (1965), 95
Highway Safety Act (1965), 95
Hispanics, 24, 25, 97
Hitler, Adolf, 32
Hobbes, Thomas, 17, 57, 112
Hofer, Norbert, 103
Howell, William G., 9, 10
Hungary, 100, 103, 107, 108, 115
Hurricane Katrina, 36, 137
Hussein, Saddam, 63

illiberal democracy, 15, 65, 97, 98, 99,
  100, 104, 105, 112, 116, 118, 119
Illinois, 87
Immigration and Nationality Act
  (1965), 95
impeachment, 74, 75, 136, 137
India, 107, 108
Indonesia, 107, 108
insurrection, 75, 119, 123

international relations, 27, 29, 32
Iran-Contra scandal, 36, 137
Iraq, 63, 137
Israel, 107, 108
Italy, 107, 108, 139

January 6, 2021, Capitol attack, 119, 123
Japan, 107, 108
Japanese Americans, internment of, 22
Jesus Christ, 32
Johnson, Lyndon B., 33, 70, 71, 80, 92, 94, 95, 96, 110, 133, 134, 135
Jordan, 107, 108
Juvenal, 124

Kaczyński, Jeroslaw, 103, 115
Kennedy, John F., 35, 37, 46, 110, 134
Kenya, 107, 108
Kim Jong Un, 37
King, Anthony, 20

landmark legislation, 23, 46, 80, 134
law enforcement, 75, 123, 136
LBJ. See Johnson, Lyndon B.
leadership studies, 32
Lebanon, 107, 108
Le Pen, Marine, 103, 114, 115
legislature, 14, 20, 115, 116, 117, 118, 134, 136
Leviathan, 16, 17, 18, 83, 104, 112
Levitsky, Stephen, 119
liberal democracy, 15, 65, 97, 98, 99, 100, 101, 102, 104, 105, 106, 111, 112, 115, 116, 118, 119, 121, 123, 125
Lincoln, Abraham, 3, 70, 71, 73, 134

Machiavelli, Niccolò, 13, 76, 82
Madison, James, 5, 52
Madisonian system, 23, 54, 62
Marshall, John, 61
Marx, Karl, 34
Mayer, Kenneth, 21
Medicaid (1965), 95
Medicare (1965), 95, 120
Mexico, 30, 108
middle class, 104, 105, 112, 113, 119
Moses, 37, 38, 72
Motor Vehicle Air Pollution Control Act (1965), 95
Motor Vehicle Safety Act (1965), 9
Mounk, Yascha, 106, 111
Mouton, Nico, 34
Muslims, 30, 121

National Endowment for the Humanities (1965), 95
National Institute of Allergy and Infectious Diseases, U.S., 41
national security, 49
Native Americans, 133
Neo-Nazis, 115
Netherlands, 103, 107, 108, 115
Neustadt, Richard, 9, 10, 21, 23, 27, 84, 85
New Deal (1933–1939), 49, 61, 134
New York, 87
New York City, 62
Newton, Isaac, 32
Nigeria, 107, 108
Nixon, Richard, 36, 48, 71, 74, 75, 110, 133, 135
Noah, 38

North Korea, 37
Nye, Joseph, Jr., 27

Obama, Barack, 23, 24, 25, 26, 39, 71,
   77, 79, 87, 96, 110, 121, 134, 138
Obamacare, 39, 88, 121
Office of Legal Counsel, 59
Operation Warp Speed, 42
Orban, Viktor, 103, 115
Oval Office, 16, 17, 75, 135

Paine, Thomas, 51
Palmer, R. R., 118
Parliament (UK), 136
parliamentary system, 136
Pelosi, Nancy, 123
Pence, Mike, 122, 123
Peru, 107, 108
Petry, Frauke, 103
Philadelphia Constitutional
   Convention, 6, 130
Philippines, 103, 107, 108
Plato, 32, 105
Poland, 100, 103, 107, 108, 115
political science, 32
Pollock, Jackson, 128
populism, 88, 97, 99, 101, 104, 105, 114,
   115, 119, 121, 122
post-Cold War era, 99
post-Watergate era, 87
presidential dilemma, 86
presidential election, U.S. (2016),
   30
presidential election, U.S. (2020),
   138
presidential power, 2, 7, 10, 17, 54, 61,
   63, 81, 82, 83, 84, 120

President's Daily Briefing (PDB),
   44
Putin, Vladimir, 100, 103, 155

Rasul v. Bush (2004), 59
Reagan, Ronald, 13, 49, 62, 87, 96
Reedy, George, 70, 73
republican executive, 129
Richardson, Elliot, 36
Robinson, Greg, 21
Roman Republic, 98
Rome, 58, 125
Roosevelt Room, 36
Roosevelt, Franklin D., 60, 69, 84,
   86, 96, 133, 134, 135, 138
Roosevelt, Theodore, 2, 89, 93, 96
Rosenau, James, 29
Rousseau, Jean Jacques, 112
Russia, 33, 100, 103, 107, 108, 115

Sanders, Bernie, 105
Santayana, George, 132
Schlesinger, Arthur, Jr., 84, 86
Secretary of Homeland Security,
   U.S., 25
Secretary of the Navy, U.S., 87
Senate, U.S., 4, 25, 58, 75, 95, 122, 134,
   135, 136
Senegal, 107, 108
separation of powers, 1, 5, 6, 7, 12, 13,
   14, 19, 20, 23, 24, 48, 52, 53, 55, 57,
   73, 83, 84, 102, 120, 122, 128, 136
September 11, 2001, attacks (9/11), 56,
   59, 62, 63, 64, 69, 89, 91
Shakespeare, William, 33
Shaw, George Bernard, 133
Sisyphus, 16, 17, 18, 83

smart power, 27
Smith, Richard Norton, 36
soft power, 27
Souter, David, 67
South Africa, 107, 108
South Korea, 107, 108
Soviet Union, 3, 49, 99, 117
Spain, 107, 108
Spielberg, Steven, 71
stimulus bill, 92
suffrage, 111
Supreme Court, U.S., 2, 4, 25, 59, 67, 109
Sutherland, George, 61
Sweden, 107, 108, 115
Syrian refugee crisis (2015), 115

Taliban, 62
Tanzania, 107, 108
tax cuts, 17, 92
Tea Party, 103, 105, 120, 121, 122
Texas, 87
Thompson, Dennis F., 72
Tollefson, Jeff, 40
Tolstoy, Leo, 33
Trump, Donald, 11, 30, 31, 40, 43, 48, 70, 71, 74, 75, 87, 88, 96, 97, 103, 105, 114, 115, 121, 122, 123, 133, 135, 138, 139
Tuchman, Barbara, 38
Tunisia, 107, 108
Turkey, 100, 103, 107
Twain, Mark, 132
22nd Amendment (U.S. Constitution), 137
tyrannophobia, 4
tyranny, 4, 6, 7, 23, 52, 57, 74, 89

undocumented children, 24, 25
unitary theory of executive power, 48, 49, 50, 52, 53, 54, 55, 56, 58, 59, 62, 63, 64, 65, 66
United Kingdom, 101, 103, 115, 136
United Kingdom Independence Party (UKIP), 103, 115
United States, 1, 17, 24, 25, 30, 40, 44, 47, 50, 54, 57, 59, 61, 62, 63, 75, 86, 88, 89, 92, 98, 99, 100, 101, 103, 109, 115, 121, 123, 136, 139
United States v. Curtiss-Wright Export Corp. (1936), 61
University of Southern California, 29

vaccines, 39, 40, 42
Venezuela, 103, 107, 108
Vietnam, 36, 87, 107, 108, 133, 137
voting rights, 33, 80

war against terrorism, 48, 60, 61, 62, 63
war powers, 136
Water Quality Act (1965), 95
Watergate, 36, 61, 75, 87, 133, 137
welfare state, 49
White House, 2, 10, 30, 35, 41, 62, 69, 70, 75, 77, 80, 84, 123, 132
Wildavsky, Aaron, 88
Wilders, Geert, 103
Woodward, Bob, 41
World War II, 22, 32, 60

Ziblatt, Daniel, 119

Printed in the USA
CPSIA information can be obtained
at www.ICGtesting.com
JSHW021758150724
66444JS00003B/200